The Philosophy of Group Polarization

Group polarization—the tendency of groups to incline toward more extreme positions than initially held by their individual members—has been rigorously studied by social psychologists, though in a way that has overlooked important philosophical questions. This is the first book-length treatment of group polarization from a philosophical perspective.

The phenomenon of group polarization raises several important metaphysical and epistemological questions. From a metaphysical point of view, can group polarization, understood as an epistemic feature of a group, be reduced to epistemic features of its individual members? Relatedly, from an epistemological point of view, is group polarization best understood as a kind of cognitive bias or rather in terms of intellectual vice? This book compares four models that combine potential answers to the metaphysical and epistemological questions. The models considered are: group polarization as (i) a collective bias; (ii) a summation of individual epistemic vices; (iii) a summation of individual biases; and (iv) a collective epistemic vice. Ultimately, the authors defend a collective vice model of group polarization over the competing alternatives.

The Philosophy of Group Polarization will be of interest to students and researchers working in epistemology, particularly those working on social epistemology, collective epistemology, social ontology, virtue epistemology, and distributed cognition. It will also be of interest to those working on issues in political epistemology, applied epistemology, and on topics at the intersection of epistemology and ethics.

Fernando Broncano-Berrocal is a Ramón y Cajal fellow at the University of Barcelona, Spain. He works mainly in epistemology, with an emphasis on virtue epistemology, philosophy of luck, social epistemology, and collective epistemology. He is the co-editor, with J. Adam Carter, of *The Epistemology of Group Disagreement* (Routledge, 2021). His work has appeared in such places as *Philosophical Studies, Analysis, Synthese,* and *Erkenntnis*.

J. Adam Carter is Reader in Philosophy at the University of Glasgow, UK. His expertise is mainly in epistemology with particular focus on virtue epistemology, social epistemology, relativism, know-how, epistemic luck, and epistemic defeat. He is the author of *Metaepistemology and Relativism* (2016), co-author of *A Critical Introduction to Knowledge-How* (2018), and co-editor, with Fernando Broncano-Berrocal, of *The Epistemology of Group Disagreement* (Routledge, 2021). His work has appeared in *Noûs, Philosophy and Phenomenological Research, Philosophical Studies, Analysis,* and the *Australasian Journal of Philosophy*.

Routledge Studies in Epistemology
Edited by Kevin McCain
University of Alabama at Birmingham, USA
Scott Stapleford
St. Thomas University, Canada

For more information about this series, please visit: www.routledge.com/
Routledge-Studies-in-Epistemology/book-series/RSIE

The Philosophy of Group Polarization
Epistemology, Metaphysics, Psychology

Fernando Broncano-Berrocal
and J. Adam Carter

Routledge
Taylor & Francis Group

NEW YORK AND LONDON

First published 2021
by Routledge
52 Vanderbilt Avenue, New York, NY 10017

and by Routledge
2 Park Square, Milton Park, Abingdon, Oxon, OX14 4RN

Routledge is an imprint of the Taylor & Francis Group, an informa business

Library of Congress Cataloging-in-Publication Data
Names: Broncano, F. (Fernando) author. | Carter, J. Adam,
   1980– author.
Title: The philosophy of group polarization : epistemology,
   metaphysics, psychology / Fernando Broncano-Berrocal and
   J. Adam Carter.
Description: New York : Taylor & Francis, 2021. | Series: Routledge
   studies in epistemology | Includes bibliographical references
   and index.
Identifiers: LCCN 2020045004 | ISBN 9780367901011 (hardback) |
   ISBN 9781003023654 (ebook)
Subjects: LCSH: Polarization (Social sciences) | Social groups. |
   Distributed cognition. | Knowledge, Theory of.
Classification: LCC HN18.3 .B76 2021 | DDC 306—dc23
LC record available at https://lccn.loc.gov/2020045004

ISBN: 978-0-367-90101-1 (hbk)
ISBN: 978-1-003-02365-4 (ebk)

Typeset in Sabon
by Apex CoVantage, LLC

Contents

Preface

Have you ever disagreed with your government's stance about some significant social, political, economic, or even philosophical issue? For example: healthcare policy? Response to a pandemic? Gender inequality? Structural racism? Drilling in the Arctic? Fracking? Approving or vetoing a military intervention in a foreign country? Transgender rights? Exiting some multi-national political alliance (for instance, the European Union)? The building of a 20 billion dollar wall? We're guessing the answer is most likely "yes".

Next question: have you ever deliberated about such a contentious topic with people whose views are very similar to your own, e.g., perhaps with your family and very close friends (and other like-minded people?) If so, chances are very high that we can tell you what happened next.

Bring yourself back to the situation. You enter the pub, your relatives' home, or your workplace. Maybe you appear online. Suddenly, someone brings up the hot topic, "Hey, have you heard the latest. . . ?" And a heated debate ensues. You go first and voice your opinion: "yes, I can't believe it". Following your opinion, your arguments come next. Maybe they are not the best, but you make sure your point is registered. The others follow suit: opinions are voiced, arguments are shared. As the debate unfolds, you hear new arguments and get acquainted with evidence you were unaware of, and so does everyone. More and more cards are put on the table, but all are of the same suit, and the debate intensifies. Time to cool down. "Enough politics for today", you think to yourself, so you leave the pub, your relatives' home, your workplace, or you just put your smartphone away. However, something has changed. *You* have changed. Perhaps you noticed it, perhaps you didn't, but one thing is overwhelmingly likely: you are now *more convinced* that you're right (and your argumentative opponents wrong) than before. And here comes the spoiler: *the same has happened to everyone else you talked with*.

If the above situation sounds familiar to you, then you're not alone. The phenomenon you've experienced—*group polarization*—is a very familiar one. To a first approximation, group polarization is a tendency, well-studied among social psychologists, of deliberating groups to incline toward more extreme positions than initially held, on average, by their individual members before deliberation. Widely replicated empirical studies have detected polarization effects in groups discussing a wide variety of topics, and the phenomenon is believed to feature centrally (and cross-culturally) in a high number of socially relevant phenomena such as jury decisions, political debates, financial decision making, extremism, terrorism, and—of course—interaction with like-minded people on social media.

Despite the close attention that group polarization has received in empirical psychology, the widespread tendency of groups to polarize has attracted almost no attention among philosophers. With this work, we aim—for the first time in a book-length treatment—to fill this gap. Whereas social psychologists have tried to pin down the causes of group polarization, our aim is to rigorously investigate the *metaphysics* and *epistemology* of this remarkable phenomenon in a programmatic and novel way.

Drawing from the latest empirically informed philosophical research in collective epistemology, social ontology, the metaphysics of groups, and virtue epistemology, we argue that group polarization can be epistemically virtuous but is typically a *collective epistemic vice*. A broader rationale for the book—beyond establishing its novel conclusion—is as follows: a clear understanding of the epistemology and metaphysics of group polarization is needed if we are to address further philosophical questions on safe theoretical ground, including questions concerning the ethics of group polarization, such as whether we should blame a group or its members for becoming extremist.

The empirical results of social psychology are undoubtedly illuminating for understanding the causes of group polarization, but empirical research, albeit necessary, is not sufficient for answering such philosophical questions. The task to undertake, then, is to translate and interpret the phenomenon of group polarization in terms of a language that not only philosophers can understand but that can also be put to work by allowing theorists from different philosophical disciplines to identify, formulate and address genuinely *philosophical* problems related to group polarization that remain unidentified and, therefore, unsolved.

Here is the plan for what follows. In Chapter 1, we first draw several distinctions for investigating polarization phenomena from a philosophical perspective and then provide an overview of the book's topic and goals. In Chapter 2, we outline the key characteristics of group polarization, drawing from work in empirical psychology. In Chapter 3, we pinpoint the factors that make group polarization *epistemically* adequate or inadequate. In Chapter 4, we outline two key questions about group polarization—one metaphysical (concerning its nature), the other epistemological (concerning its epistemic properties) and canvass some possible answers to the metaphysical question in terms of the distinction between reductionism (or summativism) and non-reductionism about groups. In order to shed light on the epistemological question, we explain the distinction between (i) cognitive heuristics and biases and (ii) epistemic virtues and vices as drawn in virtue epistemology and its precursor, virtue ethics. We suggest that they—i.e., a heuristic/bias model and a virtue/vice model—provide two salient and genuinely alternative ways of understanding much of our cognitive behavior, both at the individual and at the collective level. Finally, by considering possible combinations of (i) reductionism and non-reductionism (concerning the metaphysical question) with (ii) the competing heuristic/bias and virtue/vice models (in response to the epistemological question), we map *four (salient) possible ways to understand group polarization.*

In Chapters 5 and 6, we show that the views that combine non-reductionism with a heuristic/bias interpretation and reductionism with a virtue/vice interpretation are implausible. In Chapter 7, we articulate and criticize the view that group polarization is a summation of individual heuristics and biases. We do so in a way that draws from (among other things) considerations about the causes and characteristics of group polarization detailed in Chapters 2 and 3. In Chapter 8, we spell out—and provide a defense of—the view that group polarization can be understood as a collective epistemic virtue or a vice. We revisit the objections to the other views and argue that it steers clear of them. We also venture ways in which the four views might be reconciled. In Chapter 9, we suggest how the epistemic pitfalls of group polarization might be mitigated at the collective level, in light of the conclusions drawn.

The result of this short book is the first thoroughly philosophical treatment of group polarization. It is one that we hope will not only offer some reasons for adopting the collective virtue/vice view we defend here but also stimulate further philosophical work on this meaningful topic.

The authors are grateful to an inspiring conference at the University of Copenhagen (2017) on group disagreements and polarization, which initially piqued our interest in this book project (through what turned out to be much instructive disagreement about disagreement and polarization itself).[1]

Note

1. Broncano-Berrocal's contribution to this project has been supported by a 2019 Leonardo Grant for Researchers and Cultural Creators, BBVA Foundation. The BBVA Foundation accepts no responsibility for the opinions, statements, and contents included in this book, which are entirely the authors' responsibility. Carter's contribution to this project has been supported by the Leverhulme-funded "A Virtue Epistemology of Trust" (#RPG-2019–302) project, which is hosted by the University of Glasgow's COGITO Epistemology Research Centre, and he is grateful to the Leverhulme Trust for supporting this research.

1   The Philosophy of Polarization Phenomena

1.1 The Aim of the Book

Group polarization is a tendency of deliberating groups to incline toward more extreme positions than initially held, on average, by most of their individual members prior to deliberation. When a group polarizes, the average post-group response is more extreme *in the same direction* than the average of the pre-group response (Myers & Lamm 1976). The phenomenon is very well-established in social psychology, where many empirical studies have detected polarization effects in groups discussing a wide variety of topics. Outside laboratory conditions, group polarization is believed to feature centrally (and cross-culturally) in a high number of socially relevant phenomena such as jury decisions, political debates, financial decision making, extremism, terrorism, and online interaction, hence its practical and theoretical significance. However, although widely investigated in empirical psychology, this important tendency of groups has not attracted much attention among philosophers. With this book, we aim to fill this gap. Whereas social psychologists have tried to pin down the causes of group polarization, our aim is to investigate its metaphysics and epistemology in a novel and programmatic way.

In this chapter, we will state more precisely what our project is, draw some conceptual distinctions concerning polarization phenomena, and vindicate the place of philosophy when it comes to theorizing about them. We distinguish, in §1.2, polarization from extremism; in §1.3, two general senses of polarization; in §1.4, polarization from disagreement. In §1.5, we compare group polarization to belief polarization and, in §1.6, to political polarization. In §1.7, we state the two guiding questions of our investigation, and our methodological approach and vindicate the place of philosophical theorizing about polarization phenomena.

1.2 Polarization and Extremism

Moving to extremes is not the same as polarizing. Moving to extremes is compatible with shifting to any of the two poles of a given scale, whereas polarization only involves moving toward the near—or already preferred—pole (Fraser et al. 1971). Thus, when one polarizes, one also moves to an extreme, but if one moves to an extreme, one does not necessarily polarize, as one can shift to the opposite pole. Polarizing is just a way of moving to extremes.

Neither moving to extremes nor polarizing necessarily implies that one has become an "extremist". Extremism, in general, consists in adopting an extreme attitude on a given scale, and one might move slightly to an extreme (e.g., polarize) without thereby adopting what constitutes the extreme attitude on the scale. For example, if one uses the left–right political spectrum to classify someone's political views, that person's views count as extremist if they are located at any of the two poles of the scale: far-left or far-right. However, that person might only move to extremes or polarize from, say, a center-right position to a right view without yet becoming a far-right extremist. That is, one does not become an extremist until one adopts a view that is located at a pole of a given scale.

Polarizing and *shifting to the opposite pole* are the two ways of moving to extremes and hence of becoming an extremist. An individual whose political attitudes are located on the center-right of the political spectrum at t_1 and shift to far-right at t_2 becomes a far-right extremist by polarizing: that person's attitudes move toward the near or already preferred pole. By contrast, an individual whose political attitudes are located on the far-left of the political spectrum at t_1 and shift to far-right at t_2 becomes a far-right extremist by shifting from one extreme to another, i.e., *without* polarizing.

1.3 Bidirectional and Unidirectional Polarization

In the different empirical literatures—but also in several normative disciplines as well as in the media—the term "polarization" is used in two different general senses that we can characterize as follows:

> **Bidirectional polarization:** for any individual or collective agents X and Y, if at t_1 X and Y respectively hold conflicting attitudes A_1 and A_2, then X and Y bidirectionally polarize if A_1 and A_2 become more extreme toward their near or already preferred poles at t_2.
> **Unidirectional polarization:** for any individual or collective agent X, if at t_1 X holds attitude A, then X unidirectionally polarizes if A becomes more extreme toward the near or already preferred pole at t_2.

Bidirectional and unidirectional polarization apply both to individuals and groups, but the minimal number of agents involved differs. Unidirectional polarization involves at least one individual or group whose attitude becomes more extreme. By contrast, bidirectional polarization involves at least two agents, individuals or groups, whose attitudes move further away in opposite directions.

The crucial difference between them is, precisely, that in bidirectional polarization, the agents involved polarize in *opposite directions*, whereas in unidirectional polarization, they polarize in the same direction. For example, when media say that US society is polarized, what is meant is that US society is polarized *bidirectionally*. By contrast, when we say of an individual that they have become radicalized, what is meant, among other things, is that that individual has *unidirectionally* polarized toward an extreme worldview. We should keep this general difference in mind, because the same term, "polarization", is often used in these two senses to refer to importantly different phenomena.

Although it is certainly not the same to say that a group has "polarized", meaning that it has bidirectionally polarized internally, as saying that it has "polarized", meaning that it has adopted a more extreme view (i.e., unidirectionally polarized), the two senses of polarization are conceptually related in that bidirectional polarization necessarily involves unidirectional polarization but not the other way around. Saying that the conflicting attitudes, A_1 and A_2, of two agents bidirectionally polarize is conceptually the same as saying that A_1 and A_2 unidirectionally polarize in opposite directions. However, an agent's unidirectional polarization is not an instance of bidirectional polarization unless there is another agent whose attitude unidirectionally polarizes in the opposite direction. Unidirectional polarization is accordingly more fundamental, at least conceptually.

1.4 Polarization and Disagreement

Disagreement can be classified in many ways. One way is in terms of whether it involves collectives or individuals. For example, *interpersonal disagreement* occurs when two or more individuals disagree amongst themselves. Those individuals can be members of different groups but, in interpersonal disagreement, individuals do not disagree in their capacity as group members but as individuals. Groups can disagree too: *intergroup disagreement* occurs when two or more groups disagree between them. Intergroup disagreement can involve disagreement between individuals, too, but, in such a case, the individuals who disagree do it in their capacity as group members and, specifically, as spokespersons for their groups. By contrast, *intragroup disagreement* is the kind of disagreement that occurs within a group between individual group members or subgroups of that group. Finally, disagreement can also take place between an individual and a group (*one-versus-many disagreement*).[1]

As we can see, whatever shape a disagreement takes (whether interpersonal, intergroup, intragroup, or one-versus-many), it always involves at least two agents (individuals or collectives) whose attitudes conflict. How does polarization relate to disagreement? First, disagreement can occur without polarization, as it does in the case of agents whose conflicting views do not change over time. For example, someone with center-right views might disagree with someone with center-left views on, say, economic policy without their views shifting a bit in any direction. Such individuals disagree but do not become more polarized. In fact, disagreement can occur with *de*polarization. Someone with far-right views might hold a disagreement with someone with far-left views on economic policy; upon discovering their disagreement, they might conciliate and shift, respectively, to center-right and center-left positions while still being in disagreement.

Even if disagreement and polarization are phenomena that can occur independently, disagreement between individuals, groups, or within groups that intensifies over time involves polarization. In particular, individuals, groups, or group members who disagree about some issue see their disagreement intensified when they polarize bidirectionally about that issue, i.e., when they unidirectionally polarize in opposite directions.

With all these distinctions in place, let us compare group polarization with two other polarization phenomena studied, respectively, in psychology and political science: *belief polarization* and *political polarization*.

1.5 Group Polarization and Belief Polarization

When psychologists talk about "group polarization", they mean a tendency of some groups to move to extremes following deliberation. This phenomenon ought not to be confused with a different polarization phenomenon that psychologists call *attitude*—or *belief polarization*. Belief polarization occurs when individuals who disagree about a given proposition see their own beliefs reinforced after individually assessing a body of mixed evidence that both supports and contradicts their beliefs, absent any deliberation.

By way of illustration, in an often-cited experimental study, Lord and colleagues (1979) selected some undergraduates who firmly believed that capital punishment has a deterrent effect and others who firmly believed the opposite. Subjects were asked to individually assess two fictional but realistic pro-deterrence and anti-deterrence empirical studies, as well as prominent criticisms to such studies in the alleged literature and the replies offered by the alleged authors. The result was that subjects who initially favored the position that capital punishment has a deterrent effect (i) more strongly believed it after being exposed to the pro-deterrence study and (ii) regarded it as significantly more convincing than the anti-deterrence study; the same effect, but in the opposite direction, was found in anti-capital punishment subjects. This result confirmed that all participants were biased in favor of the study that supported their initial beliefs and, more generally, the hypothesis that belief polarization is due to biased assimilation of the evidence.[2]

Let us compare group and belief polarization.

First, whereas belief polarization arises in the *absence of deliberation*—namely when subjects *privately* assess and assimilate available evidence in a biased way—group polarization arises *following group discussion*.

Second, both group and belief polarization involve individuals and groups, but whereas belief polarization is fundamentally an individual phenomenon, group polarization is fundamentally a collective phenomenon. The empirical studies on belief polarization involve mixed groups of people with similar and opposing beliefs about a given topic. However, communication is absent among them, which means that belief polarization is tested *individually*—namely, by asking subjects to read and process the relevant evidence silently, as in Lord et al. (1979). Group polarization affects groups of like-minded individuals who communicate with each other about their like-minded views, but it is tested *collectively*. In particular, group polarization is measured by seeing whether or not, and to what extent, the average of individual post-discussion responses is more extreme than the average of individual pre-discussion responses. The focus on average responses gives rise to the possibility that a group of individuals polarizes *on average* when no individual in the group polarizes (i.e., when no group member adopts a more extreme position). Fraser et al. (1971) capture this possibility as follows:

> a three person group using a seven-point scale (from 1 to 7 with a *neutral point* at 4) could have initial scores of 7, 5 and 2 and after discussion without consensus all might put down 5. At the group level, a slight move to extremity (which in this case is also polarization) has occurred in the shift from a mean of 4.67 to one of 5.00. But individually, after discussion the new positions are in two cases less extreme and not one of the subjects has adopted a more polarized position.
>
> (Fraser et al. 1971: 17; emphasis added)

Fraser et al.'s example is an excellent illustration of how collective unidirectional polarization, such as group polarization, can diverge from individual unidirectional polarization. In groups that polarize, individual members can unidirectionally polarize, too. For example, if all members of a group adopt a more extreme view about some issue after discussing it than the view they individually held before discussion, they all individually polarize in the same direction. In that case, the group will polarize too, as the average post-group response will be more extreme in the same direction than the average of the pre-group responses. However, this does not imply that if a group unidirectionally polarizes and adopts a more extreme view than it had, on average, before deliberating, its members will individually, unidirectionally polarize as well. This is what the example shows.

1.6 Group Polarization and Political Polarization

Another polarization phenomenon that is distinct but related to group polarization is *political polarization*. Political polarization refers to the kind of disagreements and divisions toward *ideological poles* that exist in the political life of democratic societies. As theorized in the political science literature, political polarization—sometimes misleadingly referred to as group polarization (e.g., Iyengar & Westwood 2015)—comes in two guises, depending on who is the subject of polarization: *elite popularization*—i.e., polarization among political elites (e.g., among elected party members and relevant non-elected members)[3]—and *mass* or *popular polarization*, i.e., the kind of political polarization that divides large parts of society over controversial issues, especially in the context of elections.[4]

The distinction between elite and mass polarization far from exhausts the array of polarization phenomena that falls under the umbrella term "political polarization". For example, Bramson and colleagues (2017) usefully give a (non-exhaustive) list of nine polarization phenomena dubbed "political polarization" in the social sciences, with a particular focus on formal models of opinion polarization. Relatedly, as an illustration of the ambiguity of the term in the political science literature, there is no agreement on how to define "mass polarization". As Lelkes (2016) helpfully points out, one way of conceptualizing mass polarization is in terms of how different parties and their followers are perceived to be polarized (*perceived polarization*). Others put it in terms of how much the different ideologies distribute, as a matter of fact, toward opposing poles among people (*ideological divergence*)—or else in terms of how consistently people align themselves with the different ideologies in the market (*ideological consistency*). Yet, other definitions focus on how strong people's feelings toward the different parties are (*affective polarization*).

Being so ample—in that it encompasses different phenomena—political polarization has diverse social, political, and economic causes. As explained by Barber and McCarty (2015), some candidate causes of *elite* polarization include polarized electorates, changes in the mass public, gerrymandering, primary elections, internal party dynamics, economic inequality, and private campaign financing. Candidate causes of *mass* polarization include differing world or moral views, party identification, polarization among parties, partisan media, and various kinds of sociocultural characteristics (see, e.g., Abramowitz & Saunders 1998; Fiorina & Abrams 2008; Levendusky 2013).

Interestingly, the causes of political polarization have been investigated not only in political science but also in social psychology. While the former is concerned with the social, political, and economic causes of political polarization, the latter investigates the psychological mechanisms that lead to polarization in individual subjects. In particular, several psychological dynamics have been hypothesized and empirically tested by social psychologists as possible explainers of the way people engage in the kind of controversies over *factual and moral issues* that are at the center of political polarization.

Three candidate psychological dynamics have been put forward as explanations of why people polarize over *factual issues*, i.e., controversies about facts that build upon empirical evidence, such as childhood vaccination, climate change, or GMOs (see Kahan 2013 for a detailed discussion). The first hypothesis is that individuals take sides in such controversies driven by unreflective heuristics or mental shortcuts—corresponding to what is popularly known as *system 1 reasoning-style* (Stanovich & West 2000; Evans 2003; Kahneman 2003, 2011)—and, more generally, *bounded rationality*. For example, the general public's perception of risk is often fueled by emotion-driven reasoning in covariation with cultural or ideological affinities (Leiserowitz 2005; Sunstein 2006b; Marx et al. 2007; Weber & Stern 2011). The second hypothesis is that the psychological mechanism that drives people's formation of opinions in the face of factual controversy is *motivated reasoning*, i.e., modes of reasoning and processing information that are directed by non-epistemic motives or that aim to conform to goals other than truth or accuracy (Kunda 1990; Munro & Ditto 1997; Balcetis & Dunning 2006; Carter & McKenna 2020). One of the main such motives or goals is that of protecting one's identity by preserving one's cultural and ideological values (e.g., one's individualistic, authoritative, egalitarian, or communitarian values) as well as one's commitments to other people and groups sharing the same values (Cohen 2003; Sherman & Cohen 2006; Kahan et al. 2011, 2012; Liu & Ditto 2013). Finally, the third hypothesis is that people take sides over controversial factual issues in correlation with *conservative/right-wing* and *liberal/left-wing styles of thinking*. Despite some evidence to the contrary (e.g., Crawford 2012; Kahan 2013), conservatives seem to think less analytically (Yilmaz & Saribay 2016), tend to demand greater certainty in argumentation, and to be more closed minded (Kruglanski 2004), be more responsive to negative or aversive facts (Hibbing et al. 2014), be less willing to consider countervailing evidence (Nam et al. 2013), and be more inclined toward conspiratorial thinking, including conspiracies pertaining to the Covid-19 pandemic (Alfano et al. 2020).

A complementary strand of research in social psychology helps explain why polarization related to *moral issues*—e.g., whether euthanasia, same-sex marriage, drug legalization, or late-term abortion are morally right or wrong—is so entrenched and difficult to overcome. First, moral beliefs (i.e., beliefs about what is right or wrong) are among the most strongly held attitudes (Skitka et al. 2005). One explanation of this is that they are more intensely tied to emotions than non-moral beliefs (Tetlock et al. 2000;

Haidt 2001; Nucci 2001; Skitka et al. 2008), to the extent that moral disagreement can increase the social and even the physical distance between
people with opposing moral values, thus fostering intolerance (Haidt et al.
2003; Skitka et al. 2005; Wright et al. 2008). Moreover, if a group or an
authority (e.g., a court) goes against one's moral convictions, their support
for such authority tends to decrease (Mullen & Nadler 2008), which suggests that individuals are more inclined to prioritize perceived moral duties
than duties to obey authorities or comply with group norms. Finally, when
reasoning about moral affairs, we tend to fall prey to motivated reasoning:
that is, we attempt to use general moral principles to reach preferred moral
conclusions (Uhlmann et al. 2009; Ditto et al. 2009). In light of this empirical evidence, it comes as no surprise that political polarization over moral
issues is among the most entrenched forms of polarization.

Having seen how political scientists understand the phenomenon of
political polarization as well as some of its candidate causes (both in
political science and social psychology), let us compare group polarization (as theorized in the social psychology literature) and political polarization (as theorized in the political science literature).

First, political polarization is polarization over *politically significant issues* such as healthcare, environmental regulation, economic
policy, or social rights. Collective beliefs affected by group polarization can be about such politically significant issues too, but they can
be about *politically irrelevant issues* as well, such as purchase decisions or chess moves.

Also, both group and political polarization are fundamentally collective phenomena (although both involve individuals and groups). Political
polarization affects large layers of society and is observed (e.g., through
different kinds of surveys, analysis of political discourse, and analysis
of voting behavior) in groups of all kinds, including political parties,
partisan media, the electorate, or communities. Group polarization, by
contrast, is typically tested in laboratory settings for small groups, i.e.,
groups composed of a few like-minded subjects who discuss a topic. The
fact that it is observed in small groups does not mean that it does not
affect larger layers of society. For instance, as an example of group polarization at a larger scale, David G. Myers (2010)—one of the leading fig-
ures of the group polarization literature—observes that the percentage
of landslide counties in the US (those voting 60% or more for one presi-
dential candidate) nearly doubled between 1976 and 2000. This distribution plausibly has to do, according to Myers, with the fact that people
self-segregate: liberal communities attract more liberal members, whereas
conservative communities attract more conservative members, which creates echo chambers where the available information and arguments lean
in the same direction, potentially leading to group polarization.

It is thus reasonable to think that group polarization is related to political polarization in significant respects. One connection point might be

that some of the individual psychological dynamics underlying political polarization play a role in group polarization. For example, it is in principle possible that individuals in homogeneous deliberating groups fall prey to the pathological forms of bounded rationality that are characteristic of politically polarized subjects—we will consider this possibility when discussing the view that group polarization is a summation of individual biases.

However, among the leading proposed candidate causes of group polarization, we find particular group dynamics related to deliberation (see Chapter 2), not the varied political, social, and economic causes that are put forward in the political science literature as possible explainers of political polarization. To put it another way, the phenomenon of group polarization as well as its causes are more specifically circumscribed in social psychology than political polarization and its causes are in political science. After all, recall that political polarization is an umbrella term for different politically significant polarization phenomena (see, e.g., Bramson et al. 2017), while the way social psychologists define group polarization is univocal—viz., as consisting just in the average post-discussion group response becoming more extreme in the same direction than the average pre-discussion group response.

A more plausible point of connection between the two phenomena is this: group polarization contributes, in general, to the rise of tribalism (Sunstein 1999) and can, in this way, function as a *cause* of political polarization. We know from the social psychology literature that groups whose members initially lean toward the same political views (e.g., political parties, unions, activist organizations) hold more extreme views after internally discussing them. In other words, group polarization makes groups unidirectionally polarize over politically significant issues. Consequently, if the opposite political views of two given groups become more extreme after internal deliberation, the groups bidirectionally polarize in such a way that political polarization intensifies.

1.7 The Room for Philosophical Theorizing

At this point, the reader might reasonably ask: "so what is even left for *philosophers* to tell us about the different polarization phenomena that political scientists and social psychologists have not already said?" As we'll see, quite a bit!

To bring this point into focus, let us consider, more specifically, the key question concerning group polarization around which the research agenda of social psychology has mainly revolved:

> **Descriptive Question:** what causes a group to lean toward a more extreme view after group discussion than the view held, on average, by their members before deliberating?

In pursuing an answer to this *purely descriptive question*, social psychologists have not only repeatedly confirmed the existence of group polarization—e.g., Sunstein (2002: 177) describes it as one of "the most robust patterns found in deliberating bodies"—but, as we will see in the next chapter, they have also proposed several competing descriptive hypotheses about the group dynamics and mechanisms that cause groups to polarize. In this way, the empirical studies conducted have attempted not only to confirm the existence of group polarization but also to single out the factors that the proposed hypotheses identify as the *key causes* of the phenomenon.

However, even if the empirical evidence about what causes the phenomenon is rock-solid, moreover, *even if we knew everything that has to be known about the causes of group polarization*, two crucial philosophical questions about the phenomenon remain unclear, namely a *metaphysical* and an *epistemological question*.

Before formulating these two questions, we would like to note that the kind of project we are undertaking—i.e., investigating the philosophical aspects of a well-established empirical phenomenon to answer relevant philosophical questions—is commonplace in philosophy. By way of illustration, consider a classical philosophical question: "does free will exist?" Libet's famous experiments (Libet et al. 1983) showing subjects make conscious decisions *after* having performed the actions the decisions are about have typically given a negative answer to this question (e.g., Wegner 2002). Consider another question: "is there such a thing as moral character?" Some philosophers have used empirical studies in situationist social psychology to cast doubt about its existence (e.g., Doris 1998). "Are thoughts with first-person content (e.g., bodily self-ascriptions) immune to error through misidentification?" The rubber hand illusion and delusions such as somatoparaphrenia have been put forward as empirical counterexamples to this idea (e.g., Lane & Liang 2011). "What is the nature of attention? Is conscious experience necessary for it?" Some have argued that the phenomenon of blindsight demonstrates that attention is possible in the absence of consciousness (e.g., Kentridge 2011), while others have denied it (e.g., Prinz 2011). Finally, "What are the philosophical implications of the widespread phenomenon of implicit bias?" This is becoming an increasingly popular evidence-based topic in philosophy (e.g., Brownstein & Saul 2016).

Polarization phenomena—while not a traditional concern of philosophers—have recently become the focus of the general trend of investigating philosophical aspects of well-established empirical phenomena. In particular, their nature and their philosophical implications are increasingly making waves in the philosophical literature. For example, Kelly (2008) investigates the bearing of *belief polarization* on the epistemology of disagreement by addressing whether or not it is reasonable to respond to the evidence in the way the disagreeing subjects of belief polarization experiments do. Relatedly, Hallsson (forthcoming) investigates the implications of belief polarization and politically motivated cognition for the different available ways to define the notion of "epistemic peerhood" and, in turn, for the epistemic significance of disagreement more generally. Similarly, Robson (2014) argues that empirical research on belief polarization undermines the normative claim that we should not form aesthetic beliefs based on testimony. Besides, drawing on the strand of research in the social sciences that provides formal models of bidirectional collective polarization[5] and, in particular, drawing on a formal model of agent-based deliberation, Singer and colleagues (forthcoming) have made a case for the philosophical claim that epistemically rational agents can produce bidirectional forms of collective polarization (such as *political polarization*). Finally, concerning *group polarization* (i.e., unidirectional collective polarization)—which is the topic of this book—although some philosophers discuss it in passing (e.g., Tosi & Warmke 2016; Levy forthcoming), very little dedicated philosophical work has been carried out. A notable exception is the work of Cass Sunstein—as far as his work has appeared in philosophy journals (e.g., Sunstein 2002, 2006a). Other exceptions include an attempt to model the phenomenon in Bayesian terms (Olsson 2013, forthcoming)[6] and an attempt to connect group with moral polarization (Arvan 2019).[7]

Our approach to group polarization is more ambitious than previous philosophical research, in that we aim to investigate, in a programmatic way, two important philosophical aspects of the phenomenon that researchers in philosophy have yet to address: *the metaphysics and epistemology of group polarization*. In particular, the two questions that will guide our investigation in this book are the following:

> **Metaphysical Question**: can group polarization, understood as a phenomenon that affects the epistemic lives of groups, be reduced to epistemic features of their individual members?
> **Epistemological Question**: regardless of how the metaphysical question is answered, is the epistemology of group polarization best understood in terms of a cognitive heuristic/bias model or else in terms of an epistemic virtue/vice model?[8]

Since the metaphysics and epistemology of group polarization is *uncharted territory in philosophy*, our methodology will consist in venturing several possible answers—and corresponding answer-combinations—to the two previous questions. The idea will be to pair answers to the metaphysical question with answers to the epistemological question in order to devise *four candidate ways to model group polarization from a philosophical perspective*. With these models of group polarization in hand, we will proceed to evaluate their problems and prospects. As it will turn out, the best way to account for the metaphysics and epistemology of group polarization is in terms of (i) irreducibly collective features of groups as opposed to reducible to individual features along the metaphysical dimension and in terms of (ii) epistemic virtues and vices as opposed to cognitive heuristics and biases along the epistemic dimension. The resulting proposal accordingly identifies and defends the view according to which group polarization is (typically) *epistemically vicious* and (on occasions) *epistemically virtuous*, where the relevant epistemic virtues and vices are understood in reliabilist, irreducibly collective terms.

The following idea drives our methodological approach to the metaphysical and epistemological questions. While these questions are philosophical, their answers and the philosophical views that follow need to be assessed, not only for theoretical fruitfulness but also for *empirical adequacy*—just like the views that result from answering philosophical questions such as "Is there such a thing as moral character?" or "Are thoughts with first-person content immune to error through misidentification?" need to pass an empirical check. In this sense, our investigation of the metaphysics and epistemology of group polarization will pay special attention to empirical research in social psychology, to the extent that we will sometimes adjudicate between competing views on empirical grounds—of course, as per usual in philosophy, we will also adjudicate between views on purely theoretical grounds.

Why investigate the metaphysics and epistemology of group polarization anyway? Because only by coming up with a clear understanding of the metaphysical and epistemological aspects of the phenomenon we will be able to address further important and pressing philosophical questions on safe theoretical ground. These include a cluster of questions concerning the ethics of group polarization, such as whether we should blame a group or its members for becoming extremist, and if so, what kind of rationale would be available to us for doing so.[9]

The empirical results of social psychology are undoubtedly illuminating for understanding the causes of group polarization, but empirical research, albeit necessary, is simply not sufficient for answering such philosophical questions. The task to undertake, then, is to translate and interpret the phenomenon of group polarization in terms of a language that not only philosophers can understand but that they can also put to work to identify, formulate and address genuinely philosophical problems related to group polarization in their fields, problems that remain unidentified and therefore unsolved. This book is an illustration of this kind of approach, and beyond the value of specific arguments and ideas we might offer, the more general ambition to lay the ground for further philosophical research is, we hope, the most significant *philosophical* outcome of what is to follow.

Notes

1. One-versus-many disagreement can happen within a group because the individual is a member of the group with whom she disagrees (which is a special

case of intragroup disagreement) or between a group and an individual who does not belong to it (which is a special case of intergroup disagreement).

2. Subsequent empirical studies have further confirmed this hypothesis, e.g., Miller et al. (1993), who amended some methodological deficiencies in Lord et al.'s original study. Besides, belief polarization occurs quite independently of the content of the relevant polarized beliefs, e.g., it has also been observed in beliefs about legalized abortion and environmental preservation (Pomerantz et al. 1995) or John F. Kennedy's assassination (McHoskey 1995).

3. See Layman et al. (2006) and Hetherington (2009) for two reviews of the elite popularization literature.

4. See Fiorina and Abrams (2008) for a review of the mass polarization literature; see also Hetherington (2009).

5. For a review of this literature, see Bramson et al. (2017) and O'Connor and Weatherall (2017).

6. See Pallavicini et al. (forthcoming) for a surprising consequence of this model: that under a broad range of circumstances Bayesian agents bidirectionally polarize. See Olsson (forthcoming) for discussion.

7. Arvan's view, more specifically, is that groups polarize around moral issues because individuals have a metaethical vice: the vice of conceiving moral truths as discoverable in some way, either by intuition, rational argument, theorizing, and the like. For discussion of Arvan's view (note 7 in Chapter 5).

8. We are not presenting this dichotomy as exhaustive of the possibility space but rather as capturing two salient epistemological alternatives. For instance, one might be tempted to inject a third model: rational versus non-rational belief. While we grant the logical space for this and potentially further epistemic divisions (as well as for interesting connections between them), we think the way we have framed the epistemological question picks out the two most salient kinds of description-types of group polarization from an epistemological point of view. Concerning the rational versus non-rational belief dichotomy, it is an open question whether or not group polarization, albeit perhaps being rational at the individual level, is epistemically irrational at the collective level. For example, certain characterizations of group polarization treat it as an individually rational phenomenon, such as Singer et al. (forthcoming), who reach this conclusion drawing on an agent-based model of group polarization, or Sunstein (1999), who argues that members of polarized groups might be considered rational—although it is unclear whether practically, epistemically, or both—when making assessments on the basis of the arguments offered by other group members or when trying to protect their reputation within the group. Singer et al. (forthcoming) and Sunstein (1999), however, seem to disagree about whether group polarization can be considered rational from a collective perspective. Although our philosophical investigation of group polarization is *not* concerned with group rationality, the issue of rational versus non-rational belief comes up, to a limited extent, at various points in our comparison of the two models we have chosen for particular focus. For example, the problem of Mandevillian intelligence that we put forward in §5.2.3 illustrates this kind of individual versus collective rationality disconnect from the other side of the coin: irrationality at the individual level can lead to rationality at the collective level.

9. See the individual blamelessness problem in §5.2.2 for some insights on collective responsibility.

2 The Psychology of Group Polarization

Group polarization was first discovered in the context of decision making when James Stoner (1961) observed that, after deliberation, the average of the choices of business students concerning a financial decision leaned toward a riskier decision than the average of their individual choices prior to discussing the issue. These "risky shifts" have been successfully replicated for a wide variety of groups and choices, such as purchases (Woodside 1972), professional decisions (Siegel & Zajonc 1967), negotiations (Rabbie & Visser 1972), and even chess moves (Myers & Lamm 1976). While this early research initially suggested that group polarization consisted in a mere risk-taking tendency of groups, other empirical studies (e.g., Moscovici & Zavalloni 1969; McCauley et al. 1973) soon after revealed that group choices become more *cautious* if the prevalent pre-deliberation choice of individual members tends toward caution instead.[1]

This points to the two main features of group polarization. First, it typically occurs in groups whose members engage in some sort of *deliberative process*. In this respect, polarized groups are such that the post-deliberation group attitude becomes significantly more extreme than average pre-deliberation individual judgments.[2] Second, in order for group polarization to arise, a *leaning toward the same position* must be dominant among individual members before deliberating. This *average* position (e.g., concerning some choice or decision) is precisely what is enhanced after group discussion.

Group responses are liable to group polarization cross-culturally and across many diverse deliberative contexts, which is an indication of just how generalized the phenomenon is. To get a feel for this level of generality, let's consider a few examples. Following deliberation, groups tend to hold stronger political views than those initially held by their individual members (Moscovici & Zavalloni 1969). It has also been observed that group racial attitudes become stronger after already prejudiced members discuss racial issues (Myers & Bishop 1970). Group polarization also affects how groups perceive persons, positively or negatively. For example, in a faculty evaluation task, post-discussion group ratings were more negative than pre-discussion individual ratings when the latter were on average negative and more positive when they tended to be positive (Myers 1975).

Also, one particular strand of empirical research has focused on jury decisions. As it turns out, mock jury deliberation produces more extreme judgments of guilt (as well as of innocence) depending on whether the initial tendency of mock jurors is pro-guilt or pro-innocence (Myers & Kaplan 1976). This effect is particularly notable if mock jurors have high or low authoritarian inclinations (Bray & Noble 1978). Deliberation between mock jurors also yields higher punitive damage verdicts (Schakde et al. 2000). While most empirical research has been carried out in laboratory settings, group polarization has also been detected in real courts. For example, data collected revealed that the likelihood of Federal judges to opt for extreme courses of action significantly increased if they engaged in group discussion (Main & Walker 1973). More generally, group polarization is believed to be the cause of the intensification of social conflicts following deliberation as well as of many extremist tendencies in politics (Lamm & Myers 1978; Schkade et al. 2000; Sunstein 2009).[3]

So what are the *causes* of group polarization? Quite a few have been posited, but there are three central accounts in the psychological literature. According to *persuasive arguments theory*, group polarization is primarily an informational phenomenon caused by the impact of informational exchanges on group members during collective deliberation (Burnstein & Vinokur 1977; Brown 1986). More specifically, Burnstein and Vinokur's hypothesis is that, when a group is faced with two alternatives, there is a pool of (typically culturally given) "pro" and "con" arguments (as well as other relevant information) that individual members retrieve to decide which alternative is to be favored. Depending on the quantity and quality of the arguments individually retrieved for each alternative, the group's pre-deliberation dominant attitude favors one alternative or the other. However, since not all members retrieve the same arguments, collective discussion ensures that everyone is exposed to new information in the direction of their own positions, which are thus reinforced. Since individual members hold on average a more extreme view, the group's attitude unsurprisingly becomes polarized.

An alternative explanation uses the tools of *social comparison theory*, whose fundamental assumption is that individuals evaluate their own opinions and abilities by comparison with the opinions and abilities of others, to the point that they tend to perceive and present themselves in ways that are socially desirable to others.[4] Given this assumption, group polarization is explained as follows. In group settings, individuals first estimate the group average concerning an opinion. Subsequently, they tend to perceive themselves as more extreme than the estimated average— they thus individually underestimate the real group average. During collective deliberation, this particular social comparison process prompts (a majority of) members to present themselves as more extreme than the initial group average, which means that everyone is exposed to a distorted group norm according to which the more extreme position suddenly becomes collectively acceptable.

On one version of social comparison theory, group members who initially believed that their position was more extreme than the average discover that this is not the case. While this initially causes disappointment, their desire to *obtain social approval* leads them to conform to the distorted group norm and re-adjust their beliefs to the collective view (Jellison & Riskind 1970). On another version of the theory, group members believe that their preferred option was more extreme than would have been considered acceptable by the group. Upon discovery of the distorted group norm, they are subsequently no longer concerned about *avoiding social censure*, which motivates them to adopt the extreme view (Levinger & Schneider 1969).[5]

A third notable social-psychological account of the causes of group polarization is based on *social identity theory*, whose central tenet is that social identities are constructed within the social group people belong to (the "ingroup") in opposition to other imagined or real social groups (the "outgroups"). Building on this idea, *self-categorization theory* (Turner 1982; Turner et al. 1987, 1989) explains group polarization as a phenomenon that arises in *intergroup* contexts. More specifically, group polarization is understood as conformation to a polarized ingroup norm that results from a process of self-categorization among group members when confronted with other groups' views. The idea is that this confrontation enhances group membership and self-identity in a way that minimizes *intra*group differences and maximizes *inter*group differences. The bottom line, then, is that the group polarizes because its members try to preserve their distinctiveness from other groups.[6]

Notice that while persuasive arguments theory maintains that group polarization arises because of *informational influences*, social comparison theory and self-categorization theory instead posit that it arises due to *normative influences*. Interestingly, as Kelly et al. (2013) have noted, the processes described by persuasive arguments theory and by social comparison theory are *individually sufficient* to give rise to group polarization. In particular, groups can polarize when group members are exposed to arguments and evidence supporting the group's dominant attitude in the absence of information about the positions of other group members (Sanders & Baron 1977). And conversely, groups can polarize when group members have information about the positions held by other members even when no arguments or evidence for the dominant position is available (Goethals & Zanna 1979). In any case, the three psychological theories are supported by empirical evidence (see Isenberg 1986 for a review), which suggests that they might not be strictly incompatible accounts after all and that, in typical cases of group polarization, *both* informational as well as normative influences are at work (see Lamm & Myers 1978 for further discussion).

While the psychological literature is filled with studies that aim to determine how and why groups polarize, there is comparatively less empirical research specifically devoted to the mechanisms of *group depolarization*. Nonetheless, insofar as the three main psychological theories identify several factors as the determinants of group polarization—namely, informational influences, social comparison, and self-categorization mechanisms—these theories (at least indirectly) predict that the absence of such factors would contribute to group depolarization.

Concerning *persuasive arguments theory*, Vinokur and Burnstein (1978) show that in groups with equally opposed subgroups, deliberation tends to decrease the distance between the subgroups due to *informational influences*. This is what they call "depolarization", but note that it is not exactly the opposite of group polarization, understood as an increase in the group's average belief. In particular, what Vinokur and Burnstein's studies indicate is that while the distance between the two subgroups decreases following deliberation, the average belief of the whole group still increases, i.e., the group still polarizes, albeit less significantly than in groups without this subgroup structure. The reason for this is that, even if groups internally organized into opposed subgroups tend to polarize less than otherwise, disproportionate informational retrieval (i.e., as when an individual attends to a greater extent to pooled information/arguments that align with a previous tendency) can still occur with the consequence that the group as a whole still polarizes. This idea is explained by Vinokur and Burnstein (1978) as follows:

> [W]e know that on issues that shift toward risk, there exist more prorisk arguments than pro-caution arguments; vice versa on issues that shift toward caution; and on neutral (non-shifting) issues, the number of prorisk and precaution arguments is evenly balanced. As a result, during discussion of a risky item, the prorisk subgroup will have more supporting arguments available than the precaution subgroup; the reverse should be the case in the discussion of a cautious item; and, of course, with a neutral item, each subgroup ought to have a similar number of supporting arguments available.
>
> (Vinokur & Burnstein 1978: 878)

Studies reported by Turner et al. (1987) also lend support to the predictions of *self-categorization theory* concerning group depolarization. In particular, according to Turner and colleagues, such studies offer evidence that "when divisions are made salient, mutual influence within the group as a whole will be inhibited, assuming no strong pressures to reach agreement" (Turner et al. 1987: 161). In other words, making transparent to subjects that the group is internally divided into two subgroups triggers a comparison mechanism among subgroups that in turn makes it more likely that the group depolarizes (in Vinokur and Burnstein's sense, i.e., depolarization as subgroup convergence) than when such a divide is not made salient.

Finally, psychological studies on depolarizing mechanisms also indicate that, as we would expect, eliminating the enabling conditions for *social comparison* has a depolarizing effect. Abrams and colleagues (1990), for example, have reported that (i) providing conditions for *private* (i.e., non-observed by group members) responses by individuals decreases ingroup influence, and (ii) further, that experiments demonstrating that when categorical differences between subgroups within a discussion group are made salient, convergence of opinion between the subgroups is inhibited (Abrams 1990: 113–114).[7]

Notes

1. See Myers and Lamm (1975) for relevant discussion on how the literature on the risky-shift effect was reinterpreted as an instance of the more general phenomenon of group polarization.
2. Empirical research (e.g., Teger & Pruitt 1967) has detected group polarization effects after merely exposing group members to the views of other members. However, the detected polarizing effects are *much less significant* than if they engage in group discussion.
3. For a more detailed discussion of political polarization, see Chapter 1.
4. See Festinger (1954) for the original proposal of this influential approach to social psychology.
5. See Burnstein and Vinokur (1977), Isenberg (1986), Lamm and Myers (1978), and Pruitt (1971) for relevant discussion of social comparison theories.
6. See Krizan and Baron (2007) for discussion on the limitations of this approach.
7. See Sunstein (2000) for a review of further factors that contribute to group depolarization, including unfriendliness among group members, physical distance, confidence, lack of solidarity, or obscure matters of fact being discussed.

3 The Epistemology of Group Polarization

3.1 Group Polarization and Group Belief

Empirical research on group polarization is mainly concerned with detecting polarization effects in a wide variety of contexts, such as in jury decisions, negotiation behavior, ethical decisions, risk assessment, judgments, and attitudes toward an array of political, religious, and social matters or online interaction. For the purposes of philosophical discussion, we can naturally consider cases of *polarized group judgment* (e.g., about political, religious, or social matters) as cases of *polarized group belief* or (more weakly) *group acceptance*.[1]

Moreover, the same applies in the case of *polarized group decisions*. To see this, note that it is generally the case that one chooses or decides to ϕ only if one believes or at least accepts that ϕ-ing is one's choice or decision. We should not suppose that group choices or decisions are any different. After all, just consider that the way many studies try to detect polarized group choices is by explicitly asking subjects to choose the best or the most acceptable decision, i.e., to choose what they *believe* to be the best or most acceptable decision.

Cases of *polarized behavior* are also reducible to cases of group belief. After all, in empirical studies on polarized behavior, subjects are typically requested to take action only after discussing their positions with other individuals, i.e., after discussing what they *believe* the best or most acceptable course of action would be.

Putting this all together, we can see how group polarization has straightforward epistemic import: polarized choices, decisions, and actions stem from polarized beliefs. Moreover, this result should come as no surprise. A critical feature of group polarization is that it typically befalls following deliberation, and deliberation is a process in which one expresses one's opinions and beliefs and weighs them up against the opinions and beliefs of others.

3.2 The Epistemic Neutrality, Goodness, and Badness of Group Polarization

It is standard in social psychology to class some group phenomena as *process losses*, i.e., actions, operations, or dynamics that prevent groups

from reaching their full potential.[2] Process losses have practical consequences, such as underperforming as a group in collective tasks due to *social
loafing*—viz., the reduced effort of individuals when working in group
settings compared to when working alone (cf., Paulus & Dzindolet 1993).
Other process losses have specifically *epistemic* consequences, such as the
group's making less accurate collective judgments due to *shared information bias* in *hidden profile* situations—viz., the tendency of groups to only
discuss information that most group members possess when information
privately possessed by individual members or only shared by a few of
them is more relevant than the former to make an accurate group judgment (cf., Stasser & Titus 1985).

Group polarization has epistemic consequences too, but it is far from
straightforward whether we can label them process losses, at least not
from an epistemic perspective. For example, a reason to treat group
polarization as an epistemically bad phenomenon is that groups whose
members lean, on average, toward a *false* proposition (e.g., that Earth is
flat) see this (initially epistemically bad) leaning then exacerbated after
discussion due to group polarization. This seems to make such groups
less reliable than most of their members would be if they judged the relevant issue alone, which is a sign that it is a process loss after all. However,
a reason to consider at least some cases of group polarization epistemically good or appropriate is that groups of Bayesian agents polarize (cf.
Bordley 1983; Olsson 2013, forthcoming). Bayesian reasoning is, after
all, a standard of rationality.

So how can we tell then the epistemically good cases of group polarization from the bad ones? In general, there is nothing intrinsically right or
wrong (given epistemic standards) in the fact that an individual or collective agent unidirectionally polarizes. Consider the individual case. You
merely suspect *p*—or have low credence in *p*—and encounter evidence
for *p*. This makes you believe *p* or assign higher credence to *p*. You have
in such a scenario unidirectionally polarized given a scale of propositional attitudes that ranks belief over suspicion (see, e.g., Carter et al.
2016) or given a scale of subjective probabilities. However, there is nothing *intrinsically* (epistemically) right or wrong with such polarization; the
mere fact that you have changed your doxastic attitude or mental state
is an epistemically neutral phenomenon. Instead, the epistemic goodness
or badness of your newly acquired belief or higher credence—rather than
coming from the mere fact that you have polarized—is determined by the
epistemic status of the factors that make you polarize, such as the fact
that you have encountered supporting evidence. Thus, *if your evidence is
good evidence*, it may good that you have polarized; if your evidence (or,
perceived evidence) is bad, it may be bad.

We should not suppose that group belief works any differently, i.e.,
we should not assume that there is anything intrinsically right or wrong
epistemically in the fact that a group unidirectionally polarizes. That a

collective belief polarizes is better understood as an *epistemically neutral phenomenon*, just as individually shifting from suspicion to believing or assigning higher credence to a proposition is—in and of itself—epistemically neutral. It is a neutral feature of groups' epistemic lives, just as the latter are neutral features of our individual cognitive makeup.

As in the individual case, it is the particular *way* that groups polarize— viz., the *epistemic status of the factors that give rise or contribute to it*— that determines whether group polarization is an epistemically good or bad phenomenon when it is. And this is an observation also by Sunstein (2006a: 205), who claims that "nothing in the phenomenon of group polarization demonstrates that deliberation will lead to blunders".

Accordingly, in what follows, we will not make the mistake of asking whether group polarization, as such, is epistemically good or bad. Rather, we aim to pin down the factors that lead polarized groups to blunders (or to avoid them), and, more importantly, we will elucidate the epistemic status of such factors. The resulting taxonomy of epistemically good and bad cases of group polarization will set the baseline for assessing the philosophical views that we will present and review in subsequent chapters.

3.3 Epistemically Appropriate Group Polarization

Consider an epistemically faultless case of group polarization:

> GOOD SCIENTISTS. The scientists comprising a medical research group individually collect evidence bearing on the hypothesis *H* (e.g., that childhood vaccination is safe). After an exhaustive and reliable investigation, each individual scientist finds different bodies of high-quality supporting evidence for *H* and no good evidence against. Each also makes sure to discard, reliably, any bad evidence, either for or against *H*. Drawing on their good private evidence (reliably noticing how good it is), all scientists individually come to believe that *H* is true. They meet, fully disclose their good evidence, and discuss it. They make sure that, during deliberation, no normative influences cloud their judgment. They make sure that all they care about is the confirmational import of the evidence put on the table (and are reliable at doing all of the previous items). Even more, the scientists make sure that everyone actively searches for good evidence against their individual beliefs about *H* and that everyone carefully examines the most plausible ways to prove *H* wrong. All are very reliable at doing this as well, and all eventually conclude that there is no plausible way to prove them wrong about *H*. As a result of this process, each scientist is individually more certain that *H* is true, and the group is on average more certain about it than it was before deliberation. The group has polarized, but it has done so in an (epistemically) *good* way: it is closer to the truth.

By "bad" evidence we mean, in general, evidence that comes from *untrustworthy sources* and *unreliable methods* such as hearsay, wishful thinking, guessing, cognitive bias, motivated reasoning, flawed experimentation, and the like, including misleading evidence, i.e., evidence that merely appears to be good or, in other words, evidence that comes from seemingly trustworthy sources or reliable methods but that in reality comes from untrustworthy sources or unreliable methods. By "good" evidence, we mean evidence from reliable methods —such as evidence produced by reliable cognitive faculties (e.g., perception, good reasoning, memory) or by scientific inquiry (e.g., meta-analyses, randomized clinical trials, cohort studies) —as well as evidence from trustworthy sources (e.g., reliable informants, peer-reviewed journals, experts). By using the common-sense qualifiers "good" and "bad", we do not mean that one cannot be rational (or reasonable) in following bad evidence. Indeed, that might be the case, especially when one's evidence is misleading.

With this caveat in mind, the question we want to now zero-in on is this: *why* is there nothing epistemically problematic about the way the scientists polarize in GOOD SCIENTISTS? Let's try to pin down the most relevant factors that seem to help the research group avoid blunders:

1. The average pre-deliberation belief is true (or approximates truth more than falsehood).
2. Group members reliably collect good evidence and reliably discard any bad evidence.
3. Group members reliably and correctly judge the confirmational import of their private evidence.
4. There is full disclosure of the privately possessed good evidence during group deliberation.
5. Group deliberation is not affected by any normative influence (e.g., social comparison or self-categorization processes) and is led by a generalized interest to notice the confirmational import of the evidence put on the table.
6. Group members reliably and correctly judge the confirmational import of the evidence shared by other group members.
7. Group members reliably search and discuss good evidence against their individual beliefs, reliably judging its confirmational import and reliably examining the most plausible ways they could be proven wrong.

The satisfaction of 1–7 plausibly jointly suffice for group polarization to be epistemically appropriate. Or course, there might be other relevant factors bearing on the epistemic appropriateness of group polarization, but good cases typically instantiate 1–7—although, as we will see, this does not mean that they are all *necessary* for epistemically appropriate group polarization (indeed, satisfying all of 1–7 might very well, in some cases, involve supererogating epistemically).

Unsurprisingly, good cases of group polarization tend to occur in areas of expertise or groups with the highest epistemic standards (such as those of science). However, it should be emphasized that even in those domains, groups still hold false beliefs, fail to filter out bad evidence, and fall prey to normative influences, cognitive biases, etc. As a result, good cases of group polarization are *rarer than bad cases*, mainly because as soon as one leaves the domain of science and expertise and moves deeper into the mire of less-epistemically driven issues such as politics, religion or morality, bad cases of group polarization become the norm and not the exception. Accordingly, for this reason, group polarization tends (rightly) to be regarded as a *negatively valenced phenomenon* (e.g., Sunstein 2006a describes it as a "deliberative failure"). Another reason, of course, is that group polarization carries unwelcome practical consequences, such as increased tribalism or even terrorism. For the sake of clarity, however, let us keep the epistemic and the practical dimensions apart.

3.4 False Pre-deliberation Group Belief

What makes a case of group polarization epistemically *inappropriate*, then? We have not spelled out necessary conditions for epistemically appropriate group polarization, so we cannot point to a failure of one such condition as a clear-cut way to explain why a given case is a bad case. That said, factors 1–7 are nonetheless *typical* (perhaps necessary) conditions of epistemically appropriate group polarization. We can accordingly distinguish different ways in which group polarization can go epistemically wrong by parsing each of these factors and the epistemic implications of their non-obtaining.

Thus, one way in which group polarization can fall short of epistemic adequacy is that the average pre-deliberation belief of the group is false (or approximates falsehood more than truth). Group polarization merely accentuates the initial leaning of a group. That is not per se epistemically inappropriate. However, if that inclination is already toward a false and hence epistemically inadequate view (e.g., that Earth is flat), group polarization will provide further epistemic disvalue by moving the average attitude closer to that falsehood. This does not mean, of course, that reliable or competent groups cannot form false average pre-deliberation beliefs and polarize following deliberation—we will return to the issue of group reliability in Chapter 8 (e.g., in §8.2.2.). This doesn't mean that if the dominant view of a group is true, group polarization becomes epistemically good. As it turns out, other factors can render group polarization an epistemically bad phenomenon, as we will see next.

3.5 Filtering of the Evidence

During deliberation, group members either share their private evidence with other members or they do not. Sharing or not sharing evidence is itself something group members might or might not be aware of (e.g., it might be due to a conscious decision or to an unconscious process). However, independent of that, *the very process of sharing/not sharing evidence* can be assessed epistemically along the following lines: a group member's evidence-sharing process is epistemically appropriate only if it does not facilitate bad evidence entering group discussion. Call this epistemic constraint, for short, *successful filtering*.

Successful filtering (i.e., not letting bad evidence enter, de facto, group discussion) is compatible with sharing good evidence, but it is also compatible with sharing no evidence whatsoever. Group members who are reliable at acquiring good evidence will typically not let bad evidence enter group discussion. However, being reliable at obtaining good evidence is not required for only sharing good evidence on a particular occasion and hence for successfully filtering bad evidence. For example, a group member might come across good private evidence by luck and share it. Moreover, as far as successful filtering is concerned, group members can even be incompetent or perhaps unwilling information-*gatherers* while at the same time reliable at filtering their bad evidence: all they need to do is suitably recognize that they are in possession of impoverished evidence when they are and avoid spreading it to the group.

It follows from the foregoing that successful filtering is different from reliable filtering. This introduces another dimension of assessment of the evidence-sharing process: a group member's evidence-sharing process is epistemically appropriate only if the group member is *reliable* at not letting bad evidence enter group discussion. Call this *reliable filtering*.

As in the case of successful filtering, being reliable at not letting bad evidence enter group discussion is related to—but ultimately independent from—being reliable at acquiring good evidence. Of course, a group member who only gathers good evidence and shares it with the rest is also de facto reliable at not letting bad evidence enter group discussion. However, reliable filtering is also satisfied by someone with a policy never to share her private evidence, where this person might or might not be a reliable information-gatherer. After all, reliable filtering, recall, involves reliability at *not sharing bad evidence*, not at *sharing good evidence*. In any case, the most common cases of reliable filtering are, for sure, cases in which group members possess both good and bad evidence and reliably share their good but not their bad evidence.

A final epistemic dimension of assessment, as far as evidence sharing is concerned, concerns the fact that reliable group members might prevent bad evidence from entering group discussion only *by luck*, as opposed to due to an exercise of their filtering capacities. To see this, consider first an example of lucky successful filtering *without* reliable filtering:

> COIN TOSS. A group discusses whether a certain proposition (e.g., that childhood vaccination is safe) is true or false. An unreliable group member runs a quick Google search and encounters some

evidence, but ignores whether it is good or bad. She tosses a coin to decide whether or not to share it with the rest. As a matter of luck, it is good evidence (she got it from a scientifically informed website), and she shares it. Alternatively, it is bad evidence (she got it from an anti-vaxxer website), and she does not share it. In both cases, she successfully (but luckily) prevents bad evidence from entering group discussion.

Now consider a case of lucky successful filtering *with* reliable filtering.

> SOFTWARE BUG. A group discusses whether a certain proposition (that childhood vaccination is safe) is true or false. A group member reliable at not distributing bad evidence acquires misleading evidence, but she reliably notices it. Group discussion is computer-mediated in the following way: group members first need to upload all their evidence to the cloud and then click either on "Share evidence with the group" or "Do not share evidence with the group". Once everyone has done this, group discussion begins. Reliable as she is, the group member in question clicks on "Do not share evidence with the group" to avoid feeding group discussion with what she knows is bad evidence. Unfortunately, a bug in the group discussion software triggers the bad evidence to be shared. However, as luck would have it, an IT support technician just so happens to notice the bug and turns the status of the group member's evidence to "Unshared" right away, before it has the chance to reach fellow members.

Unlike in COIN TOSS, in SOFTWARE BUG, the group member's filtering of the evidence is successful *and* reliable. The two cases have in common that in neither case is the successful filtering of the evidence successful *because of* reliable filtering. After all, in both cases, the fact that bad evidence does not enter group discussion is just a matter of luck (in COIN TOSS, good luck compensates for the lack of reliable filtering; in SOFTWARE BUG, bad luck thwarts the exercise of reliable filtering).

Both cases reveal a further dimension of assessment of the evidence-sharing process: a group member's evidence-sharing process is epistemically appropriate only if the group's member bad private evidence does not enter group discussion because she *reliably* prevents it from entering group discussion. Call this *anti-luck filtering*.

To recap: three forms of filtering are necessary (and plausibly jointly sufficient) for the epistemic adequacy of a group member's evidence-sharing process:

1. *Successful filtering* (when group members do not let bad evidence enter, de facto, group discussion).
2. *Reliable filtering* (when group members are reliable at not letting bad evidence enter group discussion).

3. *Anti-luck filtering* (when group members do not let bad evidence enter, de facto, group discussion because of exercising their filtering capacities).

Accordingly, the question that naturally arises is whether group polarization becomes epistemically inadequate when group members fail to filter their bad private evidence (i) successfully, (ii) reliably, or (iii) successfully because of reliable filtering. Before answering this question, let's take a brief detour in order to sharpen a point that's cropped up behind the scenes in the previous discussion—but that we have not made fully explicit yet—and that will put us in a better position to move forward.

3.6 Acquiring Evidence Versus Distributing Evidence

In the case of groups, different epistemic standards apply to how the evidence is *acquired* and how it is *distributed* (see Greco forthcoming for this kind of view). If individual reliability has any bearing on the epistemic appropriateness of group discussion, the fact that group members are reliable at acquiring good evidence renders group discussion epistemically appropriate in a different (albeit related) sense than the fact that group members are reliable at not distributing bad evidence within the group. How does this bear on the epistemic goodness or badness of group polarization? To answer this question, consider the following case:

> NOT-SO-GOOD SCIENTISTS. The scientists comprising a medical research group are in the business of individually collecting evidence bearing on the hypothesis *H* (e.g., that childhood vaccination is safe). But they are not very reliable at collecting *good* evidence. Each scientist randomly accumulates different bodies of evidence from both reliable and unreliable sources (e.g., meta-analyses, randomized clinical trials, biased anti-vaxxer studies, comments from pro-vaccination online discussion groups, etc.). In this way, some scientists acquire good evidence for *H*, others bad evidence for *H*, others bad evidence against *H*, and yet others evidence that is simply irrelevant. Despite this chaotic process of evidence acquisition, they make sure to discard, reliably, any irrelevant evidence they find along the way but, more importantly, any bad evidence they acquire, either for or against *H*. Those scientists with good private evidence (a majority of them) draw on that evidence (reliably noticing how good it is) and come believe that *H* is true. The rest, reliably noticing that their evidence is not good, suspend judgment. All scientists meet, fully disclose their good evidence, and discuss it. They make sure that, during deliberation, no normative influences cloud their judgment. All are exceptionally reliable at doing that, indeed, and those who suspend judgment on *H* come to believe that *H* is true after carefully and

reliably examining the evidence shared by their colleagues. Carefully and reliably examining the shared evidence is not enough, however. They all make sure that everyone actively searches for good evidence against their individual beliefs about H and that everyone carefully examines the most plausible ways to prove them wrong. All are very reliable at doing that too, and all conclude that there is no plausible way to prove them wrong. As a result of this process, each scientist is individually more certain that H is true, and the group is on average more certain about it than it was before deliberation. The group has polarized, but in a good way: it is closer to the truth.

Like the researchers of GOOD SCIENTISTS, the not-so-good scientists polarize in a way that brings their group closer to the truth. The two research groups share factors 1–7, except for factor 2, which they share partially. Recall: factor 2 involves group members reliably collecting good evidence and reliably discarding any bad evidence. The scientists in GOOD SCIENTISTS do *both* of these things; the not-so-good scientists only the latter. That is, only the former are reliable at, specifically, collecting good evidence. The question is: should this epistemic difference lead us to conclude that group polarization is epistemically appropriate in GOOD SCIENTISTS but inappropriate in NOT-SO-GOOD SCIENTISTS? The short answer is "no", but arriving at this conclusion requires carefully spelling out the relationship between acquiring and distributing evidence.

When it comes to polarized groups, we can evaluate two separate things: (i) how the evidence is *distributed* before and during group discussion and (ii) how the evidence is *acquired* before distribution. Let's consider now the relationship between the two. First, acquiring good evidence is necessary for distributing good evidence: if no good evidence enters the group, no good evidence enters group discussion. However, acquiring good evidence is not sufficient for distributing good evidence: group members who are unreliable at filtering the evidence they acquire might only acquire good evidence, fail to notice that their evidence is good, and subsequently fail to share it.

Second, acquiring bad evidence is necessary for distributing bad evidence: if no bad evidence enters the group, no bad evidence enters group discussion. However, acquiring bad evidence is not sufficient for distributing bad evidence: reliable members at filtering the evidence they acquire might only acquire bad evidence, notice that it is bad, and avoid sharing it.

Third, the latter kind of case also shows that acquiring good evidence is not necessary for bad evidence *not* being distributed. Besides, acquiring good evidence is not sufficient for bad evidence not being distributed either—group members might acquire both good and bad evidence, unreliably filter the bad evidence, and spread it to the group—unless group members *only* acquire good evidence.

Fourth, acquiring bad evidence is not necessary for good evidence *not* being distributed: group members might collect only good evidence but not share it, e.g., for strategic reasons. Besides, acquiring bad evidence is not sufficient for good evidence not being distributed either—group members might acquire both good and bad evidence, reliably filter the bad evidence, and share only the good evidence—unless group members acquire *only* bad evidence.

In sum, then, the relationship between acquiring and distributing evidence can be summarized as follows: acquiring bad evidence (i) is necessary for distributing bad evidence; (ii) it is sufficient for good evidence *not* being distributed just in case all the acquired evidence by the group is bad. Likewise, acquiring good evidence (i) is necessary for distributing good evidence; (ii) it is sufficient for bad evidence *not* being distributed just in case all the acquired evidence by the group is good. The other possible connections needn't hold.

3.7 Differences in the Quality of the Evidence

Let's now return to our example cases featuring the good and the not-so-good scientists. Both research groups reliably *prevent* any bad evidence from being distributed and thus entering group discussion, and so both use reliable mechanisms for filtering bad evidence. Does it matter that the good scientists' evidence is exclusively good, whereas the not-so-good scientists' is both good and bad evidence?

As we've seen, obtaining only good evidence (i.e., as in GOOD SCIENTISTS) is sufficient for bad evidence not being shared. By contrast, the acquisition of good *and* bad evidence (i.e., as in NOT-SO-GOOD SCIENTISTS) does *not* necessarily lead to bad evidence *not* being distributed. Here it all depends on the group's filtering mechanisms: whether or not these filtering mechanisms actually prevent bad evidence from entering group discussion. Consequently, differences in the quality of the evidence acquired by two groups are epistemically significant for considering the fact that they polarize epistemically appropriate or inappropriate, only if the filtering of the bad evidence transpires less reliably in one group than in the other. However, in the cases under consideration, both research groups would never let any bad evidence enter group discussion, and so the initial difference in the quality of the acquired evidence is not going to be epistemically significant vis-à-vis deeming one case of group polarization epistemically adequate and the other not.

And note that this point is entirely compatible with the fact that the good scientists polarize *more* than the not-so-good scientists because the former share more good evidence during group discussion. Indeed, group polarization is epistemically better in the former case because the good scientists polarize more and thus get closer to the truth by drawing on more good evidence than the not-so-good scientists. However, the comparatively greater magnitude of the good scientists' polarization does not make the polarization of the latter epistemically problematic. After all, the not-so-good scientists also get closer to the truth reliably and drawing solely on good evidence.

In more realistic and non-idealized group settings, however, a pre-discussion pool of evidence composed of both good and bad evidence (like in NOT-SO-GOOD SCIENTISTS) will typically lead to *less* reliable filtering of the bad evidence. After all, the filtering capacities of real-life groups are typically not as reliable as those of our idealized scientists, who, by stipulation, are capable of preventing *any* bad evidence whatsoever from entering group discussion. Besides, even if—in more realistic group settings—all the acquired evidence is *guaranteed* (never mind now) to be good evidence (like in GOOD SCIENTISTS), unreliable filtering capacities can nonetheless potentially lead such good evidence to be interpreted mistakenly as bad, causing it not to be shared, with a resulting process loss.

The theoretical point remains, though: for any two groups discussing the same issue, differences in the quality of the evidence acquired are not epistemically significant for adjudicating between epistemically appropriate and inappropriate group polarization *if* the bad evidence is filtered out in the same reliable fashion across both cases. Given this, we can safely conclude that GOOD SCIENTISTS and NOT-SO-GOOD SCIENTISTS are both epistemically good cases of group polarization, an assessment that is compatible with also countenancing that the former is epistemically better because, by polarizing, the good scientists get the closest to the truth.

3.8 Epistemically Appropriate and Inappropriate Filtering of the Evidence

The kind of filtering of the bad evidence of good cases of group polarization (like GOOD SCIENTISTS or NOT-SO-GOOD SCIENTISTS) is *anti-luck filtering*, i.e., successful filtering *because of* reliable filtering. The next question we need to answer is this: is a case of group polarization still epistemically appropriate if group members do *not* filter the bad evidence in that way, but rather do so *merely* successfully and/or reliably?

To bring this question into sharp relief, consider a case of group polarization in which the dominant leaning in the group is toward a true proposition—*p*—and all group members:

- Privately possess good and bad evidence for *p*—the latter is, e.g., evidence from untrustworthy sources (such as clickbait websites) and unreliable methods (such as motivated reasoning).

- But no one knows whether their private evidence is good or bad.
- Yet, all simply toss a coin to decide whether or not to share their private evidence—i.e., all use the kind of randomized filtering method described in COIN TOSS—and are, therefore, unreliable at filtering their bad evidence.

With the previous caveats in place, let's now consider two versions of the case. In the first, no group member is successful at filtering their bad evidence, and, as a result, the group's discussion revolves around bad evidence for *p*. After being exposed to this body of bad evidence during deliberation, group members adopt, on average, a more extreme view about *p*. Thus, the group polarizes drawing on bad evidence, making the case an epistemically inappropriate case of group polarization. Accordingly, successful filtering is necessary to ensure that group discussion only revolves around good evidence, which is in turn necessary for proper group polarization.

In the second version of the case, group members use the same unreliable method (i.e., a coin toss) for filtering the bad evidence, but this time, by an enormous coincidence, all the evidence they share is the good evidence in their possession. It is thus just a matter of luck that the bad evidence is successfully filtered out and that the group thereby discusses and polarizes drawing solely on good evidence. However, the case is (despite the fortuitous circumstances described) nonetheless epistemically problematic. The reason is that the group members' method for filtering their bad evidence is utterly unreliable: the group could *as easily* have polarized drawing on bad evidence, as in the first version of the case.

Thus, as the thought goes, reliable filtering is necessary for epistemically appropriate group polarization. But—and here things get a bit more complex—is a case of group polarization still epistemically adequate if group members do not filter out their bad evidence *as per anti-luck filtering*, i.e., successfully *because of* reliable filtering, but only successfully *and* reliably?

To answer this question, just consider a case of group polarization in which the dominant leaning of the group is toward a true proposition *p* and all group members:

- Privately possess good and bad evidence for *p*.
- All are reliable at discriminating whether their private evidence is good or bad.
- All are thereby reliable at filtering the group's privately possessed bad evidence.

Now suppose that such a group engages in computer-mediated deliberation using the same kind of software we described in SOFTWARE BUG, i.e., one that allows group members to share or to avoid sharing their evidence by simply clicking "Share" or "Do not share." In such a group setting, all members of the envisaged group reliably scrutinize their private evidence and turn the status of their bad evidence to "Unshared", given that they realize it is bad. However—and here is the twist—as in SOFTWARE BUG, a first stroke of bad luck (a software bug) makes such bad private evidence public, i.e., accessible to other group members. But a second stroke of good luck (the intervention of an IT support technician) then corrects the situation, preventing any bad evidence from actually reaching any of them. As a result, *only* good evidence finally enters group discussion, and the group thus polarizes drawing solely on good evidence.

Question: is this latter case an epistemically appropriate case of group polarization? Note that all group members reliably process their private evidence, discriminating the good from the bad evidence, and all do their best to avoid sharing any bad evidence they might have with the rest. Of course, it is because of a fortuitous combination of factors that bad evidence does not end up entering and subsequently corrupting group discussion, and not *because* of the exercise of their filtering capacities. Still, at least from the perspective of what group members have done to contribute to having an epistemically healthy discussion, there is nothing wrong with the way they have processed their private evidence. The case accordingly strikes us as an epistemically good case of group polarization. And this positive assessment is bolstered by the fact that, except for the lucky external factors, the case is structurally equivalent to the good cases of group polarization we have discussed so far (i.e., GOOD/NOT-SO-GOOD SCIENTISTS).

Granted, a different question altogether is whether the case is epistemically appropriate as far as *knowledge acquisition or generation* is concerned. If the evaluation standard is whether the resulting group belief qualifies as collective knowledge, the answer is, most plausibly, "no". Given how luck *intervenes* in the group's belief-forming method (in a way akin to standard Gettier cases),[3] the resulting polarized belief does not qualify as group knowledge despite being reliably formed on good evidence.

Further argumentation is of course needed to establish the precise way in which epistemic luck undermines collective knowledge (cf. Barba & Broncano-Berrocal ms.), but for the purposes here it suffices to note that this kind of diagnosis is common in individual Gettier cases: Gettiered agents (at least in the standard cases) do things epistemically right in that they use reliable cognitive abilities to form their beliefs, as opposed to unreliable methods such as wishful thinking or motivated reasoning. In this way, Gettier agents are not blameworthy for forming their beliefs in the way they form them, because they use the same kind of methods we use in the good cases of knowledge.[4] Thus, Gettier cases are epistemically appropriate in that specific respect (unsurprisingly, Gettier subjects are credited with justified beliefs).[5] If there is someone or something to be blamed, those are the external lucky factors that *intervene* in the way Gettier agents' beliefs become true, which is why Gettier cases fall short of epistemic adequacy as far as knowledge generation or acquisition is concerned. The collective case is no different.

We are now in a position to draw several conclusions from the preceding discussion. First, for any two groups discussing the same issue, differences in the quality of the evidence acquired are not epistemically significant for adjudicating between epistemically good and bad group polarization if the bad evidence is filtered in the same reliable fashion in both cases. Second, the amount of good evidence distributed during group discussion can make a good case of group polarization epistemically better. Third, group polarization is epistemically appropriate (given other relevant factors of good group polarization in place) if group members prevent their privately possessed bad evidence from entering group discussion in virtue of their reliable filtering capacities (anti-luck filtering). Fourth, group polarization is still epistemically appropriate (given other relevant factors of good group polarization in place) if group members who are reliable at preventing their privately possessed bad evidence from entering group discussion filter out such bad evidence by luck (i.e., when anti-luck filtering does not hold). In such a case, the resulting polarized beliefs might not qualify as collective knowledge. Fifth, group polarization is not epistemically appropriate (given other relevant factors of good group polarization in place and absent any other appropriateness-undermining factors) if group members successfully, though not reliably, prevent their privately possessed bad evidence from entering group discussion.

3.9 Unreliable Assessment of the Confirmational Import of the Evidence

One common feature of the good and the not-so-good scientists is that they reliably and correctly judge the confirmational import of their private and shared evidence. Failing to do so has a bearing on the epistemic appropriateness of group polarization.

Just consider that there are several ways one might misjudge the confirmational import of one's private or shared evidence. For example, one might think that one's evidence—or the evidence shared by others—comes from a reliable source (e.g., a peer-reviewed journal) when, in reality, it stems from an unreliable one (e.g., an unqualified person giving an opinionated and inaccurate take on a peer-reviewed journal article)—and the other way around, that it comes from an unreliable source when in reality it stems from a reliable one. It is also of course possible that one correctly values the evidence in question as good but mistakenly concludes that it is irrelevant to the discussed issue—and the other way around, that one takes irrelevant bad evidence to be relevant. Finally, one might also correctly assess that the evidence is good and relevant but fail to recognize the *extent* to which it supports or fails to support (or confirm or disconfirm) the discussed issue.

The epistemic consequences of misconstruing the confirmational import of the evidence are at least three. First, doing so can have a negative bearing on the group members' *pre-deliberation beliefs*. For example, before group discussion, a group member might think that her good evidence for the true proposition p is bad and that her bad evidence against p is good; as a result, she would initially believe, incorrectly, that p is false. If a sufficient number of group members form false pre-deliberation beliefs due to this unreliable appraisal of their private evidence, the group's average pre-deliberation belief can turn out false. As we have seen, once a group starts with a false view, group polarization only provides further epistemic disvalue by leading the group to adopt a more extreme false view.

Second, misjudging the evidence can also have a negative impact on the *post-deliberation beliefs* of group members. For instance, consider a case in which:

- All group members initially slant toward p (e.g., all initially suspect that p is true).
- All *overestimate* the confirmational import of their private evidence, in such a way that they sell it to their fellow members as supporting p to a greater extent than it actually does.
- As a result of the previous points, all individuals in the group shift from (merely) suspecting p to believing p, and the group, thereby, polarizes.

Regardless of whether p is true or false, it should be clear that such a wrong assessment of how much the shared evidence supports the dominant view bears negatively on the epistemic adequacy of group polarization. To bring this point into sharp relief, consider a further case in which p is true and group members misconstrue the confirmational import of the shared evidence. For example, suppose that the members of a medical research group individually believe that drug X causes side effect Y but have not yet proven it. Each member conducts an observational study establishing a *correlation* between administering drug X and side effect Y but overvalues the confirmational import of the statistical evidence, interpreting instead that X *causes* Y. During group discussion, each member presents their results to the group, claiming that they've proven causation rather than mere correlation. As a result, all group members more firmly believe that X causes Y, and the resulting average group belief gets the group closer to the truth. However, the group's evidence does not license such a move and makes the group's polarization epistemically improper—i.e., even if the group belief polarizes toward the truth.

If the epistemic inadequacy of the previous case is not straightforward enough, just compare the former research group with one whose members are reliable at evaluating the confirmational import of their evidence (like the good and the not-so-good scientists). Suppose that such a group polarizes so that the resulting average belief and the magnitude of the relevant polarization are exactly the same as in the previous case. However, this time, suppose group members draw on evidence from randomized clinical trials that *prove* (by the highest scientific standards) causation between drug X and side effect Y, something they reliably acknowledge. In this case, group polarization is epistemically unproblematic.

Third, misjudging the confirmational import of the evidence can bear importantly on whether or not group members *share their private evidence* with the rest. Indeed, accurately judging the confirmational import of the evidence is necessary for reliably preventing bad evidence from entering group discussion, in that if a group member mistakenly concludes that her bad evidence is good evidence, she will probably share it with fellow members. It is also necessary for reliably sharing good evidence because if a group member believes that her good evidence is bad, she might not share it. Thus, when misconstruing the confirmational import of the evidence issues in a sufficient number of group members sharing their bad private evidence with the rest such that the average group belief then becomes more extreme because that evidence is discussed, the group thereby polarizes in an epistemically improper way.

3.10 Insufficient Disclosure of the Good Evidence

Next question: what is the epistemic significance for group polarization of *not* sharing good evidence? To answer this, let's just consider the three ways of being reliable at filtering out bad evidence we have distinguished in §3.5: (i) reliably acquiring only good evidence and sharing it with the group; (ii) acquiring both good and bad evidence and reliably sharing only the good evidence; (iii) never sharing evidence with the group, whether good or bad.

There are epistemic differences among these ways of being reliable at preventing bad evidence from entering group discussion. We have already seen the different implications of (i) and (ii) when we compared GOOD SCIENTISTS with NOT-SO-GOOD SCIENTISTS: both are unproblematic cases of group polarization, but the former is epistemically superior given that the group gets closer to the truth (the magnitude of the group's polarization is greater) by drawing on *more* good evidence during deliberation.

By contrast, (iii), the policy never to share any evidence, if sufficiently generalized among group members, will plausibly lead to a process loss in cases where the individuals involved possess evidence that is crucial to the achievement of accurate collective judgments. This kind of process loss is characteristic of "hidden profile situations" under the shared information bias condition (see §3.2) and is also in principle possible in group polarization cases.

By way of illustration, consider an epistemically impeccable group like the research group of GOOD SCIENTISTS, such that all members initially lean toward a true view; all the evidence privately possessed is good and supports this (true) initial dominant view; all group members are reliable at collecting and sharing only good evidence as well as at appraising its confirmational import. Suppose, however, that all group members *except for one* receive a threat of harm to them that will be carried out if they share any evidence whatsoever. As a result, only one member actually shares her private evidence. The group deliberates, and since the evidence shared is good and supports the dominant view, the group ever-so-slightly polarizes. The group thereby gets closer to the truth, reliably drawing on only good evidence, but it obviously *could* have gotten much closer had all the good private evidence been put on the table rather than suppressed in light of the threat.

Does the fact that this group's good private evidence is not *fully* disclosed—but only partially so—mean that the resulting polarization is epistemically inadequate? The answer is "no". Although the group could have performed epistemically better—as it would have were it to benefit from all and not just a small fraction of the good evidence privately possessed—this does not automatically make the group's performance epistemically problematic. After all, the threatened scientists get closer to the truth reliably and drawing solely on good evidence—albeit not as much as they could have, had they used all the available evidence.

Compare the situation here with an individual analogue case: you receive good testimonial evidence—e.g., from a reliable and trustworthy source—that there are five coins in the box; based on that evidence, you form the true belief that there are five coins in the box—or give high credence to that proposition. Your cognitive performance here is epistemically impeccable because you form a true belief on the basis of testimonial evidence that comes from an acknowledged reliable informant (and you have no undefeated defeaters, etc.). However, you could certainly have performed epistemically better. For instance, you could have opened the box and formed your belief drawing on reliable perceptual evidence that there are five coins in the box—e.g., on top of your good testimonial evidence. But this possibility surely does not mean that your former cognitive performance was epistemically problematic (inappropriate). It only makes it inferior (in the sense of not maximally as good as it could be)—epistemically speaking—but still epistemically in the clear.

The group situation we have just seen is one where all the private evidence is good evidence: failing to share some good evidence (for whatever reasons) might result in a process loss, but failing to do so would not be enough to ensure that the ensuing group polarization is epistemically bad. Things change when the group's pool of evidence also includes bad evidence. For example, in a given group situation, different pieces of bad evidence can enter group discussion, and for this reason, the group might polarize. If someone in the group has good evidence that can defeat the bad evidence during discussion, then the failure to fully disclose all the good evidence *does* make group polarization epistemically problematic.

In conclusion, whether or not failing to fully disclose the group's privately possessed good evidence jeopardizes the epistemic adequacy of group polarization depends importantly on the configuration of the group's pool of evidence, in particular on whether it only includes good evidence or instead includes both good and bad evidence and, if the latter is the case, on whether such bad evidence is ultimately tabled in the group discussion.

3.11 Unreliable or Lack of Consideration of Good Counterevidence

Consider now a group with the following characteristics:

- The pre-deliberation dominant view, *p*, is true.
- The group acquires and reliably discusses only good evidence for *p*.
- The post-deliberation view is on average more extreme in favor of *p*.

Contrary to what one might initially think, the polarization of this kind of group can still fall short of epistemic adequacy *despite* the fact that the pre-deliberation dominant view is true and that the group only discusses good supporting evidence in a reliable fashion. The reason is that there might be good evidence available that the group has not discussed and that counts against *p*. Indeed, that evidence might be such that, had group members discussed it along with their good evidence for *p*, the group would not have polarized—or they might have even suspended judgment about *p*.

By "good evidence available against *p*" we mean evidence (i) that counts against the dominant view, *p*; (ii) that derives from trustworthy sources or reliable methods; and (iii) that is roughly as easily accessible to group members as their good evidence for *p*. The rationale for (iii) is that relevant evidence against *p* that no group member is in a position to access is not evidence group members *ought* to discuss, even if potentially relevant, in a sense analogous to how no one has an obligation to ϕ if one cannot ϕ. By way of illustration, consider the following case:

> MEDICAL STUDENTS. A group of medical students is given the following class assignment: to find out whether drug X causes side effect Y. The students are expected to collect the available evidence about the topic, discuss it, and present their conclusions (as a group)

to the rest of the class. Initially, they all individually suspect that X is not the cause of Y. Together, they run a quick search in PubMed (a search engine of research papers in life sciences) and find a randomized clinical trial that concludes that no causal link has been found between administering drug X and having side effect Y. Yet, they get hungry and distracted, and the search stops there. Over dinner, they discuss the study, reliably examine the methodology, and as a result, all come to believe that X is not the cause of Y. In this way, the group polarizes drawing on good evidence, i.e., on evidence from a trustworthy source (PubMed) and a reliable method (a randomized clinical trial). However, if they had spent more time researching the topic, before or during their collective discussion, they could easily have found *another* randomized clinical trial concluding (for different populations) that there is a causal link between X and Y. Moreover, had they been more careful with their search, they would have found a meta-analysis concluding that the evidence about the topic is on the whole inconclusive and that accordingly more research is needed to establish causality between X and Y. Indeed, if they had discussed this evidence, they would have suspended judgment and not polarized.

Question: is the polarization of the group of medical students epistemically appropriate? In §3.8, we concluded that, for any two groups discussing the same issue, differences in the quality of the evidence acquired are not epistemically significant for adjudicating between epistemically good and bad group polarization if the bad evidence is filtered in the same reliable fashion in both cases. Here, however, the problem is not the quality of the evidence (i.e., the balance of good and bad evidence) but rather the omission of their having brought available good counterevidence into discussion. Our assessment here is as follows: if a group polarizes toward p drawing only (or mainly) on good evidence for p but there is good evidence against p that its members *ought* to have brought into discussion but have not—or if they discuss it but fail to see its confirmational import—the polarization of such a group is not epistemically proper.

This might initially seem too harsh a verdict, but bear with us. In the case of the medical students, for instance, the source of the relevant epistemic obligation is twofold: first, the relevant counterevidence is as *easily* accessible as their original evidence; second, the students are, it should be stressed, *expected* to research the topic thoroughly.[6] Be that as it may, *whatever* factor generates an obligation to bring good counterevidence into group discussion, if the group does not discuss it and polarizes— even still reliably drawing on good evidence—the group's polarization is nonetheless problematic; it is problematic *not* because of something they have done, but more precisely because of something they *ought* to have done but did not. Indeed, the point plausibly generalizes to any evidence a group ought to discuss (i.e., not just counterevidence): when such evidential obligations are in place, failing to acquire such evidence (or unreliably assessing it) can become epistemically significant for adjudicating between epistemically good and bad group polarization.

This latter point has ramifications for how we should think about the epistemic differences between cases like GOOD SCIENTISTS and NOT-SO-GOOD SCIENTISTS. In §3.8, we argued that the fact that only the good scientists reliably collect good evidence is not such that it should lead us conclude that NOT-SO-GOOD SCIENTISTS is epistemically problematic—which, we argued, is compatible with claiming that the good scientists' polarization is *more* epistemically appropriate. We are now equipped to supplement the explanation offered in §3.8 with the following expanded diagnosis: the good evidence that the not-so-good scientists fail to acquire is evidence that they might do well to discuss, but it is not such that it is evidence that they *ought* to discuss. In the context of scientific discovery, recently discovered evidence (or evidence discovered for the first time or evidence not discovered yet) is simply not—even in according with the highest scientific standards and professional research norms—evidence that research groups ought to be in possession of or familiar with, as opposed to well-established evidence in a relevant field of inquiry that everyone working in the area *should* know. For example, a cardiovascular surgeon ought to know that damage in the aorta can lead to a quick death. Not bringing this fact into consideration when discussing with colleagues the risks of a delicate heart transplant is prudentially but also epistemically negligent. By contrast, a surgeon is not expected to know the latest developments in the treatment of a rare tropical disease (or of a new pandemic virus for that matter). Accordingly, not tabling such information for group discussion is not negligent—since, plausibly, the lack of relevant social expectations *excuses* the surgeon, both prudentially and epistemically. Likewise, the epistemic adequacy of a group's omission to discuss certain pieces of good evidence is best understood as conditional on relevant epistemic obligations (whether they are grounded on social expectations—e.g., Goldberg 2017—or on something else) being in place.

3.12 Normative Influences

So far, we've analyzed the implications of reliably and unreliably acquiring and distributing good and bad evidence for group polarization's epistemic adequacy. In other words, we have analyzed the *epistemic features* of polarized groups. The thought that groups polarize in light of epistemic influences at play (good or bad ones) is consistent with *persuasive arguments theory*, which treats group polarization as a purely informational phenomenon caused by the evidential exchanges that take place during group discussion and, in particular, by the fact that all the information and arguments brought to the table by group members slant toward the same view, viz., toward the group's dominant pre-deliberation view.

However, although group polarization can arise when only *evidential influences* are in place (see Chapter 2), groups also polarize due to *normative influences*. As we have seen, two psychological theories pin down these normative (i.e., non-epistemic) influences. According to *social comparison theory*, groups polarize in the following way: when the dominant pre-deliberation view is disclosed during deliberation, individual desires and social pressures arise—e.g., the desire or the pressure to obtain social acceptance or to avoid social censure—which lead group members to polarize in the same direction. For *self-categorization theory*, group polarization results from a process of self-categorization among group members, who come to know, during deliberation, that nearly everyone in the group shares the same view. By comparing this majority view with other groups' views, they adhere even more closely to this dominant group position (and in doing so minimize intragroup differences and maximize intergroup differences).

According to both social comparison and self-categorization theory, the factors that effectively drive groups to polarization are *non-epistemic*. And it is precisely because they are non-epistemic that they turn group polarization into an epistemically problematic phenomenon. This point should be uncontroversial: an analogous sort of epistemic inappropriateness is thematically very important in individual-level epistemology. When we form beliefs based on what we desire or what pleases us or change views because an enemy or opponent believes the same we do or simply out of prejudice or implicit bias, such beliefs do not enjoy positive epistemic status, and a salient reason for this is that they are *unreliably formed* beliefs. The very same reasoning applies to the normative influences present in many polarized groups (apropos social comparison theory and self-categorization theory): groups whose polarization is driven by non-epistemic factors are unlikely to reach true collective judgments. If they so happen to reach them (because the pre-deliberation view is true), they do so in an epistemically improper way. Compare: we also—sometimes luckily—form true beliefs by wishful thinking, but the fact that wishful think leads to true beliefs on some occasions does not mean that it is ever an epistemically proper way to form individual-level beliefs.

Non-epistemic factors can also influence *evidence sharing* and, in particular, whether group members spread bad evidence to the group. For example, group members might share their bad private evidence for strategic reasons. They might do so in order to undermine the leadership of some other member, or to gain power, or with the sole intention of epistemic sabotage. When such non-epistemic factors are in place, bad evidence (if any) is not going to be filtered out reliably. And, as before, the upshot is that group polarization in such cases will be epistemically defective.

3.13 Taking Stock

By this point we've now analyzed in detail the main epistemic factors that make group polarization cases epistemically good or bad. As it turns out, group polarization is not only a complex psychological phenomenon. It is a complex *epistemic* phenomenon as well. Let's now summarize our main findings:

1. Polarized group judgments and decisions—and even polarized behavior— can be treated as instances of polarized group belief (at least for the purposes of philosophical discussion) (§3.1).
2. There is nothing intrinsically (epistemically) good or bad about an individual or collective agent's unidirectionally polarizing. Rather, it is the way groups polarize—viz., the epistemic status of the factors that give rise or contribute to their polarizing—that accounts for whether a given case of group polarization is epistemically good or bad (§3.2).
3. There are epistemically good cases of group polarization. They tend to occur in groups with the highest epistemic standards and/or expertise (such as Bayesian agents or in some excellent cases of scientific research teams). Seven factors jointly suffice for epistemically appropriate group deliberation (§3.3):

   (i) The average pre-deliberation belief is true (or approximates truth more than falsehood).
   (ii) Group members reliably collect good evidence and reliably discard any bad evidence.
   (iii) Group members reliably and correctly judge the confirmational import of their private evidence.
   (iv) There is full disclosure of the privately possessed good evidence during group deliberation.
   (v) Group deliberation is not affected by any normative influence (e.g., social comparison or self-categorization processes) and is driven primarily by a generalized interest to ascertain the confirmational import of the evidence put on the table.
   (vi) Group members reliably and correctly judge the confirmational import of the evidence shared by other group members.
   (vii) Group members reliably search for good evidence against their individual beliefs about the issue under discussion and reliably examine the most plausible ways to disprove them.

4. Group polarization can go wrong epistemically when the average pre-deliberation belief of the group is false (or approximates falsehood more than truth). Group polarization generates further epistemic disvalue in such cases by moving the average attitude closer to that falsehood (§3.4).

5. During deliberation, group members share or fail to share their private evidence with other members. This process can be fruitfully evaluated along three distinct dimensions of epistemic assessment. In particular, a group member's evidence-sharing process is epistemically appropriate only if:

    (i) *Successful filtering*: it does not let bad evidence enter group discussion.
    (ii) *Reliable filtering*: the group member is reliable at not letting bad evidence enter group discussion.
    (iii) *Anti-luck filtering*: the group member's bad private evidence does not enter group discussion because she *reliably* prevents it from entering group discussion (§3.5).

6. When it comes to group polarization, we can evaluate two things: how the evidence is distributed before and during group discussion and how the evidence is acquired before distribution. Acquiring bad evidence is:

    (i) Necessary for distributing bad evidence.
    (ii) It is sufficient for good evidence not being distributed just in case all the acquired evidence by the group is bad.

Likewise, acquiring good evidence is:

    (i) Necessary for distributing good evidence.
    (ii) It is sufficient for bad evidence not being distributed just in case all the acquired evidence by the group is good (§3.6).

7. For any two groups deliberating about the same issue, differences in the quality of the evidence acquired are not epistemically significant for adjudicating between epistemically appropriate and inappropriate group polarization if the bad evidence is filtered in the same reliable fashion in both cases. This is compatible with the fact that the amount of good evidence distributed during group discussion can make a good case of group polarization epistemically better (§3.7).

8. Group polarization is epistemically appropriate (given other relevant factors of good group polarization in place) if group members prevent their privately possessed bad evidence from entering group discussion in virtue of their reliable filtering capacities (anti-luck filtering) (§3.8).

9. Group polarization is still epistemically appropriate (given other relevant factors of good group polarization in place) if group members are reliable at preventing their privately possessed bad evidence from entering group discussion filter out such bad evidence by luck (i.e., when anti-luck filtering does not hold) (§3.8).

10. Group polarization is epistemically problematic (given other relevant factors of good group polarization in place and absent any other appropriateness-undermining factors) if group members successfully but do not reliably prevent their privately possessed bad evidence from entering group discussion (§3.8).
11. Misjudging the confirmational import of the evidence can have a negative bearing on the group members' pre-deliberation and post-deliberation beliefs as well as on whether or not group members share their private evidence with the rest (§3.9).
12. Whether or not failing to fully disclose the group's privately possessed good evidence jeopardizes the epistemic adequacy of group polarization depends on the configuration of the group's pool of evidence and in particular on whether it includes only good evidence or else both good and bad evidence, and, if the latter is the case, on whether such bad evidence ultimately enters group discussion (§3.10).
13. The epistemic adequacy of a group's failure to discuss certain pieces of good evidence depends on the epistemic obligations in place. Accordingly, if a group polarizes toward *p* drawing only (or mainly) on good evidence for *p* but there is nonetheless good evidence against *p* that its members ought to have brought into discussion but have not—or if they discuss it but fail to see its confirmational import—the polarization of such a group is not epistemically proper (§3.11).
14. Non-epistemic factors (such as social comparison and self-categorization processes) can lead groups to polarize. When this happens, group polarization is epistemically inadequate (§3.12).

Notes

1. For recent discussion of these issues, see for example Brady and Fricker (2016).
2. See VandenBos (2007) for this definition of process loss.
3. For discussion of intervening epistemic luck, see, e.g., Pritchard (2005), and Broncano-Berrocal and Carter (2017).
4. This point can be of course challenged, see, e.g., Broncano-Berrocal (2017, 2018).
5. However, see Williamson (2016) for a dissenting view here, on which Gettier subjects are claimed to be unjustified, in virtue of merely believing but not knowing, though blameless.
6. Social expectations can give rise to collective obligations to discuss evidence, i.e., there is information groups might be expected to have and discuss given the kinds of groups they are (e.g., medical students, surgeons, politicians, researchers, juries, etc.; cf. Goldberg 2016)

4 Four Models of Group Polarization

Over the past several chapters, we've reached a number of conclusions. We've seen that group polarization (i) typically occurs in groups whose members engage in some sort of deliberative process and (ii) when individuals in the group antecedently lean, on average, toward the same position. Further, we've seen (in Chapter 2) that three leading candidate causes of group polarization are provided by *persuasive arguments theory*, *social comparison theory*, and *self-categorization theory*. Chapter 3 then outlined in some detail factors that bear on the epistemic appropriateness or inappropriateness of group polarization.

Let's now, against that background, revisit the metaphysical and epistemological questions posed in Chapter 1.

4.1 The Reductive and Non-reductive Models

The first metaphysical question, recall, asks whether group polarization, understood as an epistemic feature of a group, can be *reduced* to the group's individual members' epistemic features. This kind of metaphysical question is typically phrased using the language of *summativism*. Any summativist position about group features (e.g., collective responsibility, collective knowledge, the property of being corrupt, the tendency of groups to only focus on information shared by their members, etc.) is committed to the following principle:

> **The summativist principle**: necessarily, if a group G possesses a feature F, then one or more individual members of G possess F or related features of the same type.

For example, if a group is responsible or corrupt, according to the summativist principle, at least one member of the group is responsible or corrupt. In this way, what any summativist view rules out is the possibility that groups instantiate features over and above the features of individuals members, i.e., that group features "float freely" from individual features.

The summativist principle leaves open a metaphysical question concerning the extent to which group features *reduce* to the features of individual group members. There are at least two options. A permissive form of summativism (permissive in the sense that a group may count as having a feature in terms of only *one* member having it), yet a strong form of reductionism (strong in the sense that group features can reduce to features of one group member) is what we can dub *strong reductionism*, which Kallestrup (2016) defines as follows:

> **Strong reductionism:** a group G has a feature F if and only if at least one individual I is both (i) a member of G and (ii) has F.[1]

A more restrictive form of summativism (restrictive in the sense that a group counts as having a feature only if all or most members have it), yet a weak form of reductionism (weak in the sense that group features reduce to features of all or most group members) is *weak reductionism*, which Kallestrup characterizes as follows. Assuming that individuals I_1, $I_2 \ldots I_n$ are suitably organized members of group G (all or most of them), and that $F^*, F^{**} \ldots F^{+n}$ are features of the same type as—but distinct from—the group property F, weak reductionism is the view that:

> **Weak reductionism:** a group G has feature F if and only if individuals $I_1, I_2 \ldots I_n$ are both (i) members of G and (ii) have related features $F^*, F^{**} \ldots F^{+n}$.

Here is not the place to adjudicate between strong and weak reductionism in general. Strong reductionism might be true of some kinds of group features, while weak reductionism of others. For example, if a law sanctions an organization as corrupt if *at least one* individual member acts in a corrupt manner so that the organization itself is the primary and direct financial beneficiary, the property of being corrupt in this legal sense is best interpreted along the lines of strong reductionism; whether a group is corrupt in this case *reduces* to whether one group member is corrupt. In the same vein, whether a terrorist group is dangerous might come down to whether one of its operative members is dangerous (e.g., if a single operative member is in possession of a nuclear weapon). By contrast, other kinds of collective properties are better accounted for in terms of *weak reductionism*. For example, the whole collective of Liverpool supporters is not violent simply because a few Liverpool fans are violent or a university class of 100 anti-racist students is not a racist class if one student is racist. Instead, Liverpool supporters are violent or a university class racist when *all or most* of their respective individual members are violent or racist.

For our own purposes, we can rule out *strong reductionism* as a plausible candidate for modeling the metaphysics of group polarization. Here is a general argument. Suppose that feature F is a property that makes groups polarize in an epistemically inadequate way. Given reductionism, F can only be an individual (as opposed to a genuinely collective) property. In particular, F is a property such that if a group member believes p before deliberating and instantiates F, she will adopt a more extreme post-deliberation attitude toward p (or give higher credence to p) in an epistemically improper way—i.e., she polarizes precisely because she instantiates F. Now, since (social psychology tells us) group polarization consists in the average post-group response becoming more extreme in the same direction as the average pre-group response, this means that typical cases of group polarization are such that *most* (more than one) group members initially lean toward the same proposition and adopt more extreme post-deliberation doxastic attitudes *because*, ex hypothesi, they instantiate F. This is consistent with weak reductionism. It is also consistent with strong reductionism. However, the latter should be ruled out as a plausible reductionist model of group polarization. To see this, imagine a large group G such that only one member instantiates the polarizing property F. G would *not* polarize, given the previous—recall: in typical cases of group polarization most (more than one) group members need to instantiate F. Yet, strong reductionism predicts G's polarization. Since *at least* one member of G instantiates F, the view is committed to saying that G as a whole instantiates F, the polarizing property. The problem with this is that it is hard to see how a group can polarize when only *one* group member instantiates an epistemically problematic polarizing property F *unless* this is due to an *irreducibly* collective group dynamic. However, the latter is something a reductionist model of group polarization cannot accept by definition, hence why weak reductionism is preferable.

Additionally, though, there are well-known and serious problems with strong reductionism as a thesis about the properties of groups more generally, and these are worth briefly canvassing. As Alexander Bird (2019) notes, there are (at least) three such general worries, all of which can be framed in terms of the group's (epistemically relevant) property of having (or lacking) a particular belief and which reveal ways in which strong reductionism is prone to make bad predictions about group properties. The first and most well-known objection concerns cases where the members of an established group (e.g., a committee) may all have (individually) a belief without that belief being a belief of the group if the group hasn't (e.g., in light of its charter) adopted it. For example, to use a case from Margaret Gilbert (1987: 189), suppose the members of a Food Committee and the Library Committee of a college are co-extensive. It might be that "all the individuals believe that there is too much starch in the college diet". However, it is only the Food Committee that believes this, whereas the Library Committee has no opinion on the matter (Bird 2019: 3).

In the previous case, the fly in the ointment for strong reductionism is that it can easily overattribute group properties when it shouldn't in cases of organized, structured groups designed for a purpose. But there are also other kinds of structures where strong reductionism generates the wrong result via *overgeneration*. For example, take a case where "all members of a group believe *p* but for some reason deny and behave as if they do not believe *p*, each member thinking that they are the only one with this strange belief" (Bird 2019: 3). Note that, in this kind of case, strong reductionism overgenerates a group property, though this overgeneration is sourced in a different kind of reason than in the "co-extensional committee" case (see also Gilbert 1989: 257–258; Bird 2010).

Strong reductionism faces *undergeneration* problems as well. This is easily shown in cases where a group has decision-making rules that are not simple majorities. In such cases, where some members' views are afforded additional weight, it might be that a group that "comes to its views in such a manner may have a belief that is the belief of only a small proportion of the individual members of the group" (Bird 2019: 3). Yet, strong reductionism will typically undergenerate this group property when such internal decision procedures are in place, particularly when the highly weighted views are few and run counter to a popular alternative view withheld by individuals who are, by the group decision procedure, afforded substantially less weight.

Accordingly—and on the basis of the previous considerations—the *reductive model of group polarization* (one of the possible candidate answers to the metaphysical questions) is best not paired with strong reductionism but rather with the less contentious *weak reductionism*. The main tenet of this model is that whatever the epistemic features of group polarization are, they are *not* features that groups instantiate irreducibly so but features that reduce to all or most of their members having relevant features of the same type.

The competing model, the *non-reductive model of group polarization*, holds that the epistemic features of polarized groups do *not* necessarily reduce to all or most—or to any group member having relevant features of the same type—but are features that groups instantiate irreducibly so. One might think that it follows from this model that the supervenience base of group polarization does not comprise group members' features at all. However, as Kallestrup (2016) and other authors in the literature on the metaphysics of groups have noted (e.g., List & Pettit 2006, 2011), a group that irreducibly possesses a feature is compatible with that feature being supervenient on related properties of its members.[2] The resulting position, as Kallestrup defines it, is the following:

> **Non-reductionism:** necessarily, if a group *G* has feature *F*, then its individual members $I_1, I_2 \ldots I_n$ have related features $F^*, F^{**} \ldots F^{+n}$ such that necessarily any other group G^* whose individual

members $I_{1*}, I_{2*} \ldots I_{n*}$ have related features $F^*, F^{**} \ldots F^{+n}$ also has F.

With the distinction between the reductive and non-reductive models of group polarization in place, we may ask: is group polarization, understood as an epistemic phenomenon, best modeled along reductionist or non-reductionist lines? In particular, is the fact that groups polarize in ways that are epistemically proper or improper (when they are) best explained in terms of irreducibly collective epistemic features—or else in terms of the epistemic features of individual groups members? To find a clear answer to this question, we need to be clear on the epistemology of group polarization and take into account the kind of epistemic factors that make groups polarize in epistemically problematic or unproblematic ways.

Recall that in Chapter 3 we characterized group polarization as—in itself—an epistemically neutral phenomenon, in the sense that it is a neutral feature of groups' epistemic lives to adopt a more extreme attitude following internal deliberation just as it is a neutral feature of our cognitive makeup to individually shift from suspicion to believing or from low to higher credence after, e.g., talking to someone. It is the epistemic status of *the factors that make groups polarize* that renders group polarization epistemically good or bad when it is. We've pinned down a range of relevant factors, such as unsuccessful or unreliable filtering of the bad evidence, unsuccessful or unreliable assessment of the confirmational import of the evidence, or the failure to examine good counterevidence when there is an obligation to do it. These factors, which help us to distinguish epistemically proper and improper group polarization, are *general* factors—viz., not theory-laden factors—and, as such, can be potentially given different kinds of substantive glosses. In what follows we intend to explore several *theories* about what makes groups or its members fall prey to such failures, unreliability, and/or omissions.

Within individualistic epistemology, two natural candidate dispositions of individuals can lead to such epistemic failures: *cognitive biases* and *epistemic vices*. By contrast, two candidate dispositions of individuals can help us to compensate for other kinds of errors: *cognitive heuristics* and *epistemic virtues*. The collective case is really no different: cognitive heuristics and biases—on the one hand—and epistemic virtues and vices—on the other—provide two (in short) "competing models" for explaining much of our cognitive behavior, *both* at the individual and the collective level.

Our endeavor here is to see how we fare at explaining the epistemic adequacy or inadequacy of group polarization along these fault lines, i.e., either in terms of the cognitive heuristics and biases of groups and their members or in terms of their epistemic virtues and vices. These two ways to model the epistemology of group polarization thus provide two possible answers to the epistemological question set out at the beginning of the book. Moreover—and importantly—these two competing models of cognitive behavior can be conveniently combined with the two approaches to the metaphysics of group polarization distinguished already—weak reductionism and non-reductionism—in order to frame four possible and interestingly different frameworks for thinking about group polarization in philosophical terms.

4.2 The Epistemic Virtue/Vice and Cognitive Heuristic/Bias Models

Cognitive heuristics and biases—and epistemic virtues and vices—respectively provide two competing frameworks for explaining not only the epistemology of group polarization but also our cognitive behavior more generally.

4.2.1 Epistemic Virtues and Vices

Epistemic or intellectual virtues, as they are discussed within contemporary virtue epistemology, are of broadly two types. On the one hand, reasons-responsive, cross-situationally consistent *character traits* (e.g., open-mindedness, curiosity, intellectual courage, conscientiousness, or intellectual humility) are typically classed as epistemic virtues insofar as they involve some suitably specified positive orientation toward epistemic goods (e.g., truth, knowledge, understanding), including (at least) certain kinds of virtuous intellectual motivations (e.g., Zagzebski 1996; Battaly 2015) and that contribute to the agent's personal intellectual worth (Baehr 2011). Such traits are the characteristic object of focus of the *virtue responsibilism* branch of virtue epistemology. By contrast, the term "epistemic virtue" is used by *virtue reliabilists* (e.g., Greco 1999, 2003, 2010; Sosa 1991, 2009, 2015) to denote well-functioning *cognitive faculties* (e.g., perception, memory, introspection, etc.), which are themselves considered epistemic virtues (or, alternatively, cognitive abilities)[3] whenever they are truth-conducive, stable features of an individual's cognitive character[4] that are specified at a suitable level of generality.[5] Both types of epistemic virtues are meant to play a primary explanatory role in knowledge acquisition and, more generally, in epistemic evaluation.

Just as individuals manifest epistemic virtues, they also manifest *epistemic vices* (which will be important in what follows), corresponding roughly with the *virtue reliabilism* and *virtue responsibilism* dividing line. From the former perspective, epistemic vices are understood as dispositions to form beliefs *unreliably*. For example, poor memory, eyesight, and perception are epistemic vices on the reliabilist model because most beliefs formed in these ways turn out false. Here, though, an important clarification is in order: epistemic vices, no less than reliabilist virtues—and unlike cognitive biases, as we will discuss shortly—must be specified at a certain level of generality that is neither too broad nor too specific. The task of satisfying this constraint on virtues and vices is known as the *generality problem* for reliabilism. Second, regarding permissiveness: vices *must* be unreliable. For example, if it turned out that a faculty that was thought to be unreliable was in fact reliable, it would no longer be a vice, according to virtue reliabilism.[6] These further points are important when it comes to cleaving apart the distinct but related notions of epistemic vice and cognitive bias. In particular: (i) there is, unlike with vices, no constraint on the specificity of biases, and (ii) what makes something a bias is definable without reference to its reliability; thus, unlike vices, some biases can be reliable.

A different (yet compatible) way to understand epistemic vices—corresponding with the virtue responsibilist tradition—is along the lines of a *character trait* model, where epistemic viciousness is a matter of a trait's involving—or *failing to involve*—certain kinds of characteristic epistemically oriented motivations.[7] On one interpretation of the motivational component of intellectual character vice that has been gestured toward by Heather Battaly (2014: 109–110), intellectual character vices as such involve characteristically bad intellectual motivations. For example, we might think that part of what makes intellectually dishonest or narrow-minded individuals intellectually vicious is that such individuals have epistemically unworthy aims—viz., aims that involve subverting or suppressing the truth.

However, while some character traits seem to involve a positive orientation toward epistemically bad ends, other epistemically relevant character traits seem intellectually vicious, not because they are positively aimed at promoting epistemically bad ends (e.g., by involving characteristic motivations toward epistemic bads) but rather because individuals who possess such traits *lack* the appropriate kind of motivation toward epistemic goods. Incurious, intellectually lazy, apathetic, or intellectually cowardly people, for example, do not seem to be epistemically vicious on account of positively desiring epistemic bads but rather in virtue of failing to be appropriately epistemically motivated. Montmarquet (1993: 138–139), Baehr, (2011: 209) and Zagzebski (1996: 207–209) embrace this more moderate position—viz. that what is distinctive of epistemic vices as such is not that they involve any positive motivation toward epistemic bads but rather a lack of appropriate motivation toward epistemic goods. As Jason Baehr puts it, this may involve "either a straightforward lack of desire for knowledge or an insufficient concern with knowledge relative to other goods" (2011: 209).[8]

4.2.2 Cognitive Heuristics and Biases

The foregoing captures the gist of the virtue/vice model for explaining cognitive behavior. Let us turn now to cognitive heuristics and biases. Just as in virtue epistemology the notion of epistemic virtue and the corresponding notion of epistemic vice are understood in two different ways—as cognitive abilities or else as character traits—in psychology there are two different, competing ways to interpret the notion of heuristic and the corresponding notion of bias.[9]

The first, *negatively valenced* way to conceptualize the notion of heuristic, which is widespread in psychology and other disciplines (including philosophy), is due to Amos Tversky and Daniel Kahneman (1974), who conceive heuristics as fast cognitive processes or mental shortcuts that generally involve focusing on one aspect of a specific kind of complex problem while ignoring others, so that, under certain conditions (most of the times), the resulting beliefs systematically depart from some objective standard of rationality provided by logic, probability, or decision theory. Heuristics in this sense, while not necessarily unreliable, are often misapplied in situations where the rational principles of logic, probability, or decision theory should be used instead, so that, when misapplied, heuristics become "biases". For example, the availability heuristic—responsible for the availability bias—occurs when someone evaluates the likelihood of an event on the basis of immediate examples that come to mind, as when someone overestimates their chances of winning the lottery after knowing that a relative has just hit the jackpot.

According to Tversky and Kahneman, the main culprit of making subjects depart from objective standards of rationality—such as those of probability theory—is the automatic and unreflective (type-1) nature of heuristics. Relatedly, one explanation of why the use of heuristics is so extensive is that they require less cognitive effort, which comes (though not always) at the cost of less accuracy. Both ideas, the type-1 nature of heuristics and the corresponding explanation of why their use is so widespread, represent one of the central tenets of the *heuristics-and-biases program* in psychology, which, since Tversky and Kahneman's groundbreaking work, has greatly expanded the list of known cognitive biases.[10]

An alternative, *positively valenced* conception of heuristics comes from the *fast-and-frugal approach* originally proposed by Gerd Gigerenzer and Dan Goldstein (e.g., Gigerenzer & Goldstein 1996; Gigerenzer et al. 1999). This approach is in plain disagreement with the picture that emerges from Tversky and Kahneman's conception of heuristics according to which, in Gigerenzer's own words, "ordinary people are cognitive misers who use little information and little cognition and thus are largely unable to estimate probabilities and risks" (Gigerenzer et al. 1999: 27). The alternative conception they put forward is best understood in the framework of *bounded rationality*, first introduced by Herbert Simon (e.g., Simon 1982), whose key tenet is that there is a fundamental distinction between two modes of rationality: the kind of *unbounded* rationality of ideal agents who have no cognitive, time, or informational limitations and the kind of *bounded* rationality of non-ideal agents who have limited cognitive capacities and limited time and who navigate environments with limited information. One way for rationally bounded agents to overcome such limitations is to use fast-and-frugal heuristics, i.e., mental shortcuts that are "fast" "because they process information in a relatively simple way" and "frugal" "because they use little information" (Gigerenzer et al. 1999: 83).

On the fast-and-frugal approach, rationally bounded agents do not use heuristics because they require less cognitive effort, on pain of accuracy, but the idea is rather that, in specific conditions of uncertainty, heuristics can perform better than more complex strategies—and because they are more accurate in such conditions, it is rational to use them.

An example of a fast-and-frugal heuristic that, in certain conditions, can be more accurate than alternative complex methods is the recognition heuristic, according to which "[i]f one of two objects is recognized and the other is not, then infer that the recognized object has the higher value with respect to the criterion" (Goldstein & Gigerenzer 2002: 76). The recognition heuristic serves then as the starting point of slightly more complex heuristics such as the minimalist or take-the-best heuristics, which allow making reliable inferences with incomplete knowledge beyond recognition.[11]

While both the heuristics-and-biases and the fast-and-frugal approaches to heuristics and biases share the idea that mental shortcuts play a central role in the explanation of our cognitive behavior, they strongly disagree in what that role is. In particular, as one might have already inferred, the notions of rationality respectively assumed by the two frameworks are in direct competition, which correspond with different research programs. Here is Gigerenzer and colleagues:

> In our program, we see heuristics as the way the human mind can take advantage of the structure of information in the environment to arrive at reasonable decisions, and so we focus on the ways and settings in which simple heuristics lead to accurate and useful inferences. In contrast, the heuristics-and-biases approach views heuristics as unreliable aids that the limited human mind too commonly relies upon despite their inferior decision-making performance, and hence researchers in this tradition seek out cases where heuristics can be blamed for poor reasoning.
>
> (Gigerenzer et al. 1999: 28)

These, in sum, are the two main conceptions of the notion of heuristic and the corresponding notion of bias. Before comparing epistemic virtues and vices with cognitive heuristics and biases, we should note that there is an important ambiguity concerning the way the term "cognitive bias" is used in the psychological literature. In particular, the term "cognitive bias" is ambiguous between what we will call the *output reading* and a *dispositional reading*.

On the *output reading*, a cognitive bias is a *belief* that is the *result* of employing a *cognitive heuristic* under certain conditions (e.g., in the heuristics-and-biases approach, in a way that systematically departs from objective standards of rationality), where the heuristic itself is a kind of mental shortcut that it is often misapplied (heuristics-and-biases approach) or else that leads to cognitive gains (fast-and-frugal approach). For example, on the output reading, the "availability bias" is the biased belief that *results* from employing the availability heuristic. In this way, it would be a category mistake on the output reading to say that a belief is formed "through" or "because of" bias: the belief just *is* the bias. By contrast, on the *dispositional reading* (which is usually favored in discussions of cognitive bias by virtue epistemologists), the bias includes both the heuristic employed as well as the output, and on this reading it is not a category mistake to say that a belief is the manifestation of a bias (or that it has been formed "through bias" for that matter).

One must keep in mind that, given this ambiguity, the heuristic/bias model of cognitive behavior could be further divided into two sub-models. This obviously has a bearing on the metaphysics of what the model concerns (viz., group polarization), for it is clearly not the same to classify a phenomenon as a state (i.e., as a group belief) as to categorize it as a disposition (i.e., as a procedure for aggregating individual beliefs). Now, given that we aim to evaluate the epistemic appropriateness or inappropriateness of polarized group *beliefs*, but, as we have argued, it is the *way* groups polarize what makes us deem such beliefs epistemically appropriate or not, it is the *dispositional reading* that we think better accords with our theoretical aims about this collective phenomenon.

4.2.3 Epistemic Virtues and Vices Versus Cognitive Heuristics and Biases

We want to conclude this section comparing and contrasting virtues and vices with heuristics and biases with two final points of clarification. First, just as heuristics and biases are not constrained by the kind of cross-situational consistency requirement on virtues and vices (which must be grounded in stable features of the subject's cognitive character, e.g., Greco 2003, 2010), likewise, (i) heuristics and biases can (unlike vices) be—and oftentimes happen to be—*reliable*; (ii) heuristics and biases can and often are in paradigmatic cases highly specific and context-dependent (pertaining, in some cases, to very specific kinds of belief content), whereas vices are, as was noted previously, more general in their application, in a way that has been important in recent literature (as we will soon explain). For example, closed-mindedness and poor eyesight are not articulated as closed-minded-when-thinking-about-politics or as poor-vision-while-estimating-distances-in-a-hallway. What the virtue epistemologist posits when positing such vices and their corresponding virtues are traits/faculties that are general enough to (when specified at a suitable level of generality) be *cross-situationally consistent.*[12]

The second concluding point, which builds from the first, is that the aforementioned and other differences between virtues/vices and heuristics/ biases have featured importantly in the recent and contentious *situationist challenge to virtue ethics* (e.g., Harman 1999, 2000; Doris 1998, 2002; cf. Alfano 2013) and, by extension, the *situationist critique to virtue epistemology* (e.g., Alfano 2012, 2013, 2014, forthcoming).[13] At the heart of these situationist critiques is the thesis that, to the extent to which cognitive heuristics and biases are documented to influence our judgments, we should be skeptical that the kinds of global, cross-situationally consistent traits posited by virtue epistemologists (of either responsibilist or reliabilist stripes) are instantiated to the extent that virtue and vice epistemologists take for granted. And indeed, given that virtue ethicists and epistemologists are overwhelmingly non-skeptical in that they think that the traits they posit are widely instantiated and saliently explanatory of our moral/cognitive behavior, the situationist maintains that this is evidence against the empirical adequacy of the postulation of such traits.

The nub of the matter for our purposes is that virtues and vices and their associated cross-situational generality—and heuristics and biases, replete with the situational sensitivity that characterizes them—are *different* kinds of explainers of cognitive behavior, and they offer explanations that can potentially preclude each other—a point that both sides of the situationist critique to virtue epistemology take for granted when engaging with the kind of empirical argument the situationist is advancing. Call this fact about the relationship between biases and virtues the *competition thesis:*

> CT: the epistemic virtue/vice model and the cognitive heuristic/bias model offer potentially competing explanations of our cognitive behavior.

CT should not be interpreted as the thesis that all cognitive behavior is explained either by a virtue/vice or a heuristic/bias model. As we interpret it, CT countenances that most aspects of our cognitive behavior for which a virtue/vice explanation is available will also be accounted for by a heuristic/bias model—and the other way around. In addition, CT can be understood as a thesis about *individual cognitive behavior*, but the virtue/vice and heuristic/bias models can also offer competing explanations of the cognitive life of groups—or at least this is what we propose in the case of group polarization—i.e., CT can also be interpreted as a thesis about *collective cognitive behavior*. With CT and these two points of clarification in place, we are now in a position to envisage distinct frameworks for thinking about group polarization in philosophical terms.

4.3 Pairing the Models

We could simply proceed and evaluate whether the *epistemology* of groups should be better spelled out in terms of a virtue/vice or a heuristic/ bias model. However, since group polarization is a *collective phenomenon*— and, as we have seen, there are competing models for explaining the *metaphysics of collective phenomena*—we cannot simply take the latter out of the equation.

Accordingly, the different competing explanations of the epistemology of cognitive behavior and the metaphysics of group features delineate *two axes* along which we can devise several ways to model group polarization from a philosophical perspective. The first axis classifies the views in terms of whether they adopt weak reductionism about group features and the corresponding reductive model of group polarization—according to which whatever the epistemic features of group polarization are, they are not features that groups instantiate irreducibly so but features that reduce to all or most of their members having relevant features of the same type—or else non-reductionism about group features and the corresponding non-reductive model of group polarization—according to which the epistemic features of polarized groups do not necessarily reduce to all or most or to any group member having relevant features of the same type but are features that groups instantiate irreducibly so. The second axis sorts the views into the virtue/vice or else the heuristic/ bias models of collective cognitive behavior. In this way, by pairing both coordinate axes, we can come up with four general models for thinking about group polarization in philosophical terms. Schematically:

Metaphysical views about group features — Epistemological models of cognitive behavior	Weak reductionism	Non-reductionism
Heuristic/bias model	*Group polarization as a summation of individual heuristics or biases*	*Group polarization as an irreducibly collective heuristic or bias*
Virtue/vice model	*Group polarization as a summation of individual epistemic virtues or vices*	*Group polarization as an irreducibly collective epistemic virtue or vice*

Figure 4.1 The four models

As pointed out in Chapter 1, we're canvassing these four views in order to evaluate how fitting they are for explaining the metaphysics and epistemology of group polarization, which is *unexplored territory in philosophy*:

The **Reductive Virtue/Vice Model**: group polarization as a summation of individual epistemic virtues or vices.

The **Collective Heuristic/Bias Model**: group polarization as an irreducibly collective heuristic or bias.

The **Reductive Heuristic/Bias Model**: group polarization as a summation of individual heuristics or biases.

The **Collective Virtue/Vice Model**: group polarization as an irreducibly collective epistemic virtue or vice.

The way these four views will purport to (potentially) explain the metaphysics and epistemology of group polarization is, roughly, as follows. Take the reductive virtue/vice model by way of illustration. On this model, epistemically adequate group polarization is to be explained in terms of a *summation of individual epistemic virtues*, whereas epistemically inadequate group polarization is explained in terms of a *summation of individual epistemic vices*. Alternatively, consider the collective heuristic/bias model. This model will account for the good cases of group polarization in terms of an *irreducibly collective heuristic* and the bad cases in terms of an *irreducibly collective bias*. The other two views will offer their own corresponding explanations.

In order to prevent a possible misunderstanding, we should mention up front that we do not envisage these four views as positing individually necessary and jointly sufficient conditions for group polarization, i.e., we are not in the business of offering an analysis of what makes groups polarize, in the traditional sense of analysis.[14] If the empirical literature teaches us anything, group polarization is an enormously complex phenomenon that involves multiple causes, including informational influences, social acceptance desires, and ingroup/outgroup salience. Psychological theories attempt to pin down some of these factors as the principal causes of group polarization, and insofar as this is what they do, they are committed to treating such factors as necessary or sufficient (or both) for group polarization. However, there is a compelling reason not to compete with empirical psychology on this score: group polarization is an empirical phenomenon, not just a fancy concept that results from sophisticated theorizing. In this way, whatever makes homogeneous groups polarize needs to be settled empirically, not by definition.

While social psychology is concerned with the causes of group polarization, our aim is to investigate its metaphysics and epistemology. These are different projects—albeit certainly not incompatible—but complementary. We accordingly construe the four views distinguished not as analyses of group polarization but as *models* for thinking about this widespread phenomenon from a philosophical perspective, i.e., as models that help answer the two *philosophical questions* of the book in an *empirically informed way*. In particular, these four views bring together the best philosophical theories for thinking about the metaphysics of groups—reductionism and non-reductionism about collective features—with two fruitful models for thinking about individual and collective cognitive behavior (the epistemic virtue/vice and the cognitive heuristic/bias models). In this way, whether they succeed in accounting for the metaphysics and epistemology of group polarization is to be judged on theoretical grounds—of course—but also in light of the best evidence available, which in our case comes from social psychology. In fact, it is on empirical grounds that some of the views will be rejected.

In the next two chapters, we will argue that neither the collective heuristic/bias nor the reductive virtue/vice models are correct. Why think that they can be dismissed? The reason, in a nutshell, is that each of these proposals faces an intractable problem (or problems).

Notes

1. Kallestrup (2016) uses different terminology. He respectively calls "summativism", "reductive individualism", and "non-reductive individualism" the theses that we call *strong reductionism, weak reductionism,* and *non-reductionism*. In addition, Kallestrup gives his definitions in terms of properties, while we talk, more loosely (albeit more generally), about features. In this loose sense, properties, states, dispositions, competences, capacities, etc. can be considered "features".
2. As List and Pettit (2006: 89) note, any form of non-reductionism about a group feature as well as the claim that its supervenience base includes related features of group members assume that "the group's 'constitution' is put in place". What does this mean? According to List and Pettit (2006: 90):

   > That a constitution is in place among a collection of people merely means that they share certain interpersonally connected dispositions: the dispositions to follow or license certain procedures in the derivation of group judgments from individual contributions. We might think of the constitution, therefore, as yet another individual contribution on the part of the members: a contribution that consists in their possession of the appropriate dispositions.

   In this way, the supervenience base of group polarization may include, in addition to individual features of group members, the specific ways these are connected, e.g., by the informational and social mechanisms described in the empirical literature.
3. See Broncano-Berrocal (2017, 2018) for different ways to understand the notion of cognitive ability.
4. The term "cognitive character" is used by Greco (2003) in part to rule out certain kinds of meta-incoherence cases from qualifying as knowledge on the virtue reliabilist framework. In particular, the requirement that reliabilist virtues be stable features of an individual's cognitive character excludes strange and fleeting processes that reliably produce true beliefs (e.g., Plantinga's (1993) brain lesion case) from qualifying as cases of knowledge.
5. Regarding the point concerning generality, see for example Conee and Feldman (1998); cf., Alston (1995), Beebe (2004). For a recent overview and notable attempted solution to this problem, see Lyons (forthcoming).
6. This point holds as well on Cassam's form of reliabilism, which he calls "obstructivism". For Cassam, vices obstruct knowledge, and that's what's

essential to them. Though vices can include (contrary to both virtue reliabilists' and responsibilists' attitudes and processes—and not just dispositions [faculty and character]), it remains on Cassam's view that if (say) a trait one has thought to obstruct knowledge turned out not to do so, then it would thereby cease to be a vice.

7. An alternative approach is defended by Cassam (2016, 2019).
8. For an excellent discussion of these issues in the context of vice epistemology and how modeling epistemic vices relates to modeling epistemic virtues, see Crerar (2017).
9. See Gigerenzer et al. (1999: 25–29) for a historical overview of the notion of *heuristic* since its Greek origins until its current use in psychology.
10. For an illustrative infographic of all known cognitive biases, see: www.visual capitalist.com/wp-content/uploads/2017/09/cognitive-bias-infographic.html
11. See Goldstein (2009) for a helpful overview.
12. As Alfano (2012) characterizes intellectual character virtues (but also, to some extent, reliabilist epistemic virtues), they are supposed to feature, apart from the property of being (i) cross-situationally consistent, the properties of being (ii) *explanatory powerful* with respect to our beliefs, and (iii) *egalitarian*, e.g., instantiated in lots of ordinary people.
13. For a brief yet useful review of the situationist critique, see Alfano and Loeb (2014).
14. For discussion of the role of analysis in philosophical theorizing, see for example Williamson (2007, 2019).

5 The Reductive Virtue/ Vice Model

5.1 The View in Outline

According to the *reductive virtue/vice model*, when individuals in a group setting who lean, on average, in a particular direction strengthen their views in the direction they lean, following deliberation, they in doing so manifest their own (individual) epistemic virtues and vices (depending on whether the polarization at issue is epistemically good or bad). In this way, for the reductive virtue/vice model, all it takes for a group to polarize in an epistemically proper or improper way is that *all or most* members of the group systematically manifest their *individual* epistemic virtues (in the good cases) and vices (in the bad cases). Thus, on this view, saying that group polarization is an epistemically virtuous or vicious belief-forming method of a group is *just* to say that a majority of group members are individually epistemically virtuous or vicious in forming their post-deliberation beliefs, the average of which is the resulting epistemically virtuous or vicious polarized group belief—this the model's key (weakly) reductionist assumption.

On this model, epistemically adequate group polarization can be explained in terms of different kinds of (individual-level) individual epistemic virtues. One proposal is that in good cases of polarization (e.g., GOOD SCIENTISTS; see §3.3), the relevant epistemic virtues are to be conceived along reliabilist lines and, in particular, as *epistemic competences*.[1] The following is a plausible specification of such a model in light of our findings in Chapter 3:

> **Reductively virtuous group polarization:** a group G virtuously polarizes if and only if all or most members of G are individually competent at:
>
> 1. Successfully preventing bad private evidence from entering group discussion.
> 2. Correctly assessing the confirmational import of their private and shared evidence.

3. Successfully preventing non-epistemic factors from influencing group discussion.
4. Searching and discussing good counterevidence against their individual beliefs, correctly assessing the confirmational import of such evidence and examining the most plausible ways to disprove such beliefs.[2]

Accordingly, a group *G* polarizes in an *epistemically vicious* way if at least less than most of *G*'s members are individually competent at either 1., 2., 3., or 4. As we can see, this model makes it easy for a group to polarize in epistemically vicious ways, which is in keeping with the plausible idea that group polarization is, for the most part, an epistemically problematic phenomenon. By contrast, the model turns virtuous group polarization into a very epistemically demanding phenomenon, in the sense that it requires group members to be individually competent in demanding ways. However, although epistemically proper group polarization is rare, it is not that rare, and imposing such restrictive constraints on individual members seems wrong.

To sharpen this suggestion, consider a group whose members individually possess competences 2., 3., and 4. but are not particularly competent at filtering out their bad private evidence—i.e., evidence from untrustworthy sources and unreliable methods—when they have it. However, they *know* that they are not particularly competent in that respect, and, to amend the problem, they subscribe to an innovative software that reliably filters out any bad evidence coming from untrustworthy sources such as biased individual blogs, partisan online forums, or chat rooms— suppose that group discussion is computer-mediated. By using this software, the group reliably succeeds in tabling and discussing good evidence, which means that the *group* is competent at successfully preventing bad private evidence from entering group discussion. By contrast, no group member is individually competent at this. Now, since group members are individually competent in the other relevant respects and the group uses a reliable *collective* mechanism for filtering out the bad evidence, the group polarizes in an epistemically adequate manner. This shows that a purely reliabilist interpretation of the *reductive* virtue/vice model is not correct: it would rule out this and similar cases as plausible cases of epistemically proper group polarization.

Perhaps the reductive virtue/vice model could appeal to other kinds of epistemic virtues and vices. For instance, there is some temptation to draw an analogy between group polarization (as captured by the reductive virtue/vice model) and *conspiracy theories*, at least as some social epistemologists have theorized about the latter (e.g., Keeley 1999; Coady 2006; cf., Sunstein & Vermeule 2009; Cassam 2016). According to Keeley (1999, §5), for example, conspiracy theories arise out of individual vice—most notably, the vice of affording too much significance to errant data.[3] Likewise, Coady (2006) identifies the source of conspiratorial thinking—in cases of epistemically problematic conspiracy theories—in individual-level paranoia and naivety, two extremes with respect to which "realism" is proposed as the (individual-level) virtuous middle ground (2006: 10).

If we think of conspiratorial thinking of the sort that sustains widely shared conspiracy theories as a sum of individual-level conspiratorial thinking and the individual vices characteristic of it, then a natural way to read the reductive model is as submitting that group polarization is broadly analogous to such conspiracy-theory-sustaining conspiratorial thinking, viz., as a sum of individual-level vices, albeit, perhaps, different ones.[4]

By way of illustration, according to Alessandra Tanesini (2018), one particular individual-level vice that features prominently in polarized debates is what she calls *intellectual arrogance*, a trait that serves ego-defense needs and manifests in conduct in ways—including interrupting, dominating discussion, resistance to being challenged, and the like (2018: 3)—that can fuel existing intellectual divisions by means such as silencing.

One way in which intellectual arrogance at the individual level could account for group polarization on the reductive virtue/vice model is as follows. As we saw in Chapter 2, one psychological account of group polarization was social comparison theory, according to which groups polarize due to a social comparison dynamic that prompts that a majority of members present themselves as more extreme than the initial group average, thus creating a distorted group norm that makes the more extreme position collectively acceptable. Given this, one possible explanation of why individual members of groups that polarize in an epistemically inappropriate way in that they present themselves as more extreme is simply that they are intellectually arrogant. In deliberative group settings, widespread intellectual arrogance among group members leads them to impose their views on their fellow members' views. Now, since one characteristic of polarized groups is that most individual members lean, on average, toward the same position, this creates a sort of "intellectual arrogance cascade" (given the relevant social comparison mechanism) that finally makes nearly everyone in the group adopt a more extreme position than prior to deliberation—in such an intellectually arrogant environment, the minority of group members who are not intellectually arrogant also adopt the more extreme position in order to avoid social censure. This, at any rate, is one possible way in which the proponent of the reductive virtue/vice model could account for epistemically problematic group polarization, whereas epistemically unproblematic cases would be simply explained in terms of group members *not* being intellectually arrogant.

An alternative way to illustrate the commitments of the reductive virtue/vice view is within Quassim Cassam's (2018, 2019) *obstructivist* framework for theorizing about epistemic vice. On Cassam's framework, epistemic vices are character traits—but also attitudes or thinking styles— that systematically (though not invariably) get in the way of knowledge[5] by obstructing the gaining, keeping, or sharing of knowledge. An example attitude that constitutes an epistemic vice for Cassam—and one that has (like arrogance) a potential bearing on group polarization—is *intellectual insouciance*. Intellectual insouciance (hereafter, insouciance) is a posture toward truth, evidence, or inquiry manifested by one's epistemic conduct and consists in a notable lack of intellectual seriousness, flippancy about basing one's views on expert opinion/the evidence. More generally, it is a "casualness/indifference to the truth/to the need to base utterances on relevant facts" (2018: 5).

In describing concrete examples of insouciance, Cassam notes the lazy and indifferent attitudes toward the truth and expertise exemplified by pro-Brexit campaigners in the lead-up to the 2015 UK Brexit vote. Interestingly, as Murray et al. (2017) note, Brexit debates have been among the most polarizing debates in the UK. On one way of thinking—friendly to the reductive virtue/vice view—the kind of lazy and indifferent (i.e., insouciant) attitudes toward the truth that featured in these debates (e.g., the claim, on busses, that £350 million would be saved via a withdrawal from the EU and would go directly to the NHS) is endemic to the group's moving to polarizing. After all, as the thought would go, without the aforementioned kind of individually vicious attitudes toward the truth obstructing successful inquiry, individuals would be more willing to accept some of the same facts by virtue of which convergence would be a more realistic possibility.

Summing up then, at the crux of the reductive virtue/vice model, epistemically improper group polarization is best understood as a sum of individual arrogance, intellectual insouciance, and perhaps, other individual-level traits[6] that manifest in polarizing behavior. Other such vices noted in the literature include what Tanesini calls hubristic pride, what Cassam (2019) calls "closed-mindedness", what Nguyen (2018) refers to as the "systematic distrust" (2018: 1) and incredulity that characterize deeply polarized subjects.[7]

5.2 Problems

The reductive virtue/vice model faces three significant problems that challenge its proposed way to account for cases of epistemically inadequate group polarization, which are arguably the most widespread kind of group polarization. These problems are the *pessimism problem*, the *problem of individual blamelessness*, and the *problem of Mandevillian intelligence*. We will consider them each in turn.

5.2.1 The Pessimism Problem

One very challenging problem for the reductive virtue/vice model is what we can call the *pessimism problem*. If the manifestation of epistemic vice by individual group members explains epistemically inappropriate group polarization, then there must be some traits that individuals in the group have that (in order to match the profile of intellectual character vices in virtue epistemology) are cross-situationally consistent as well as vicious. But to attribute such negatively valenced global character traits to nearly *all* group members who are affected by this phenomenon is plausibly to disperse viciousness too widely. More carefully: it is implausible to suppose that all or nearly all who deliberate in group contexts are individually intellectually vicious such that each instance of group polarization must be predicated upon widely dispersed individual viciousness—polarizing effects, after all, are themselves witnessed across the spectrum of intellectual demographics (see Chapter 2).

The pessimism problem, we submit, is compatible with maintaining one sense in which epistemic vice might be widespread. It might be that all or most individuals have at least one epistemic vice. The reductive virtue/vice model, however, is predicated upon a stronger claim: namely, that there exists some individual-level intellectual vice such that (in epistemically bad cases of group polarization) all or most individuals who feature in polarized groups have *that* vice and, further, that such a vice is manifested simultaneously at the individual level when groups polarize in an epistemically problematic manner.

The previous line of objection, though, does invite a response along the following lines: this kind of widespread pessimism is, with reference to empirical social psychology (e.g., Tversky & Kahneman 1974), entirely warranted. We are, on the whole, irrational in predictable ways across a range of circumstances. Isn't this, viz., the pervasiveness of bias, grounds for thinking that epistemic viciousness is widespread? Or, to get at the worry slightly differently: given what we know about defects in human reasoning, is it really that implausible to accept that epistemic vice would be as widespread as it would have to be to account for the prevalence of group polarization?

This objection offers an important opportunity for clarification. First, evidence of widespread bias is not even *prima facie* evidence of widespread vice, partly due to cross-situational consistency reasons, as outlined in §4.2.1. In addition, it is worth emphasizing that on the virtue reliabilist model, vices are *necessarily* unreliable, whereas cognitive biases are, despite being necessarily *irrational*, often nonetheless reliable ways of forming beliefs despite flouting rational norms. Given this mismatch, the bare fact that we are largely biased, in the absence of a further premise to the effect that we are largely biased in unreliable ways, would not indicate that we are largely vicious on a virtue reliabilist model. And on a virtue responsibilist model, there is an even starker mismatch between bias and vice profiles at the individual level. Even if we are even significantly *more* biased than social psychology suggests—let us suppose, implausibly, for the sake of argument that every individual has every known bias and regularly manifests it—this strong assumption would not indicate one way or another whether intellectual character vice is widespread. This is due to a fundamental mismatch between (i) the fact that character vice is generally taken to be a matter of one's desiderative intellectual motivations, e.g., our desiring and valuing intellectual goods such as truth, knowledge, or understanding; and (ii) the unconscious nature of our biases, which often do not line up with our explicit attitudes, desires, and beliefs.

The idea that there is a mismatch between biases *qua* implicit and our explicit beliefs and desires has been defended in two different ways, lining up with two competing conceptions of the structure of implicit bias: (i) dual-process theory, and (ii) the view that biases are unconscious propositionally structured beliefs (Mandelbaum 2016). On the first kind of view (e.g., Rydell & McConnell 2006), the idea is (in short) that implicit attitudes are "handled" by a particular kind of cognitive processing, which is fundamentally associative (Type-1). With reference to the Type-1/Type-2 processing distinction (Kahneman 2011), on which Type-2 processing is propositional as opposed to associative, "crosstalk" between propositional processors and associative ones is disallowed. An implication of this model, then, is that the kinds of explicit attitudes, beliefs, and desires that make up the kind of desiderative profile that determines our intellectual character (e.g., virtue or vice, on the responsibilist model) will not *in principle* be functions of our biases given the fundamental difference in the kind of cognitive processing that determines each.

Of course, on this kind of a view, it is difficult to account for how one will ever come to change one's implicit biases through explicit beliefs, intentions, and attitudes to do so. And this is a consequence that proponents of this view are for the most part prepared to accept, viz., that biases can only be changed through changes in certain "environmental contingencies, i.e., by extinction or counterconditioning" Mandelbaum (2016: 7).

On an alternative model of the structure of implicit bias defended by Mandelbaum (2016), biases are not functions of associative processing that is distinct in kind from the type of processing that underwrites our ordinary and explicit reasoning with propositional attitudes. Mandelbaum's argument relies on the idea that the structure of implicit biases is richer than what mere associative processing can furnish. Instead, we should think of cognition as fragmented and that this fragmentation can explain the kinds of "contradictions" that feature when our implicit beliefs (for Mandelbaum: biases) co-exist in conflict with explicit beliefs, such that a change in the latter often fails to elicit any change in the former.[8] It is beyond the scope of what we can do here to adjudicate this dispute about the cognitive structure of bias. For our purposes, what is relevant is that both the dual-process model and the Mandelbaum-style model line up with the thought that unconscious biases are generally cognitively disintegrated (though this disintegration is explained differently on each model) from the kinds of explicit beliefs and attitudes of which one's desiderative motivational profile is going to be a function. And—as this rejoinder continues—it is for this reason a mistake to think that evidence that cognitive bias is widespread tells us much at all about whether epistemic vice is widespread.

Even more, though, there is a further reason to think that attributing widespread epistemic vice—at least, widespread enough to account for the prevalence of polarization—is implausible in its own right—and apart from whether such a view would be lent support from considerations about the distribution of bias. First, on a virtue responsibilist picture, widespread vice involves the attribution of widespread defects in motivation. The idea that epistemically inadequate group polarization is best explained by individual vice amounts to the idea that individuals actually are defectively motivated whenever in a deliberative group setting.

Let us consider, briefly, what this might entail in a concrete case involving a jury of individuals selected, ex hypothesi, entirely randomly. The suggestion that it is implausible on the face of it that individual vice primarily explains epistemically inadequate group polarization owes to the implausibility that *whenever* a jury polarizes in an epistemically bad way, it is because a majority of randomly selected members has defective motivations when it comes to such things as truth and knowledge. Just as it is a theoretical cost to a view in ethics if one's theory of moral motivation *overgenerates* morally defective motives, it is likewise a theoretical cost in evaluative epistemology if one's view overgenerates epistemically defective motives.[9] Of course, this theoretical cost can be overcome in ethics just as in epistemology with evidence that the relevant motives really are as the theory predicts. However—and drawing from the considerations about the previous evidence—there exists no such evidence in epistemology that we are aware of.

5.2.2 *The Problem of Individual Blamelessness*

A further problem for the reductive virtue/vice model is the problem of *blamelessness* at the individual level, a problem that can be appreciated in the context of persuasive arguments theory. Arguably, given that (as per persuasive arguments theory), in the case of group polarization, everyone is exposed to a preponderance of new information in the direction of their own positions, one is blameless for updating positively one's own credence in one's previously held information. But to the extent that one's updating one's views in this fashion is blameless, it is hard to see how it could be epistemically vicious.[10] These considerations militate in favor of thinking that, insofar as we are inclined to think of the epistemic goodness and badness of group polarization as a function of the epistemic properties of individuals, rather than in terms of collective properties, these individual properties are not (individual level) vices.

Does the previous criticism of the reductive virtue/vice model hold water? Let us consider two kinds of counterreply on behalf of the reductive virtue/vice view:

- *Counterreply 1*: reject the thesis that vices are blameworthy.
- *Counterreply 2*: accept that vices are blameworthy but then maintain that individuals who polarize are blameworthy.

Let us look at these in order, beginning with Counterreply 1. The question of whether vices are blameworthy is one that has generated some serious discussion in the literature in responsibilist vice epistemology.[11] For example, suppose that one develops certain kinds of undesirable character traits due to a bad upbringing or difficult life circumstances. They become morally vicious, reenacting some of what they unfairly experienced during formative years. Such a person, as this line of thought goes, might be morally vicious but, at the same time, not responsible for such vices given that they have an excuse. But if that is right, then philosophers are mistaken to (as is often the case) associate vices as inherent targets of reactive attitudes such as blame. The vices we have are to some extent out of our control, perhaps in a way that is akin to how the biases we have are out of our control.

There are some problems with this reasoning. First, there is an opening to press back as follows. The previous reasoning seems to rely on the supposition that whenever there is some relevant kind of causal backstory to the development of vicious character, the existence of this backstory generates an "excuse" for that character that partly depends on it and in such a way as to render that vicious character an inappropriate object of blame. This is, however, a contentiously wide view of excuses. To appreciate why, let us grant that the vicious person, in so being, violates a moral norm—a kind of "ought to be" norm: one ought not to be vicious. On one standard way of thinking about the relationship between norm violations, excuses, and blamelessness due to Williamson (2016), (i) an excuse for violating a norm renders the norm violation blameless but (ii) one has an excuse for violating a norm only if one complies with the relevant *derivative* norm. The relationship between primary and derivative norms is as follows: if a (prescriptive) norm says "do X", e.g., keep your promises, the derivative norm that is generated by this primary norm prescribes something to the effect of: "do what one would normally try to in an effort to comply with the primary norm". If you promise someone you'll be at the bank at noon, and then if you fail to make it due to a traffic jam, you at least tried to do (i.e., drive to the bank) what one disposed to comply with the primary norm would do. You failed, but you tried to make it to the bank. You have an excuse you would not have had, had you never left the couch. The excuse does not mean you failed to violate the primary norm. You still failed to show up to the bank. But the excuse renders you blameless.

On the previously mentioned way of thinking, the relevant question to ask when assessing whether one's possessing or manifesting a vice is blameworthy is whether one has an excuse for either possessing a vicious disposition or manifesting it. And this then turns on the matter of whether one has attempted to comply with the relevant primary norm—either a norm to be a certain way or a norm that says not to manifest certain kinds of dispositions.

Does the possession of a causal backstory (e.g., a difficult upbringing) constitute an *excuse* for vicious dispositions and behavior? This is, of course, a challenging question. But there is reason to think the answer, at least in light of the previous view, is "no"—at least "no" to whether such a causal backstory is sufficient for the excuse. After all, it remains an open question, given one's backstory, whether one has complied with the relevant derivative norm in any given case. In some cases, one will have done so, in others not.

The proponent of Counterreply 1 might, at this point, see a further opening. The Williamsonian account of blamelessness will de facto imply that most who are vicious are blameworthy. This is because it is plausible that most who manifest morally and epistemically defective motivations and habits are—plausibly enough—not at the same time trying not to do so. That is, most will probably not be following derivative norms that prescribe that they cultivate alternative motivations to the ones they presently have. This is especially likely in the epistemic case, when one's viciousness persists in a kind of echo-chamber (Nguyen 2018) that exerts pressure against any kind of openness to viewpoints that run contrary to those prescribed by the echo chamber.

However—and here is the opening for the friend of Counterreply 1—even if all of this is granted, it remains *possible* that there are some cases in which the vicious *do* attempt to comply with the relevant derivative norm, even when there are both internal and external pressures not to do so. Here it is worth considering the case of American actress Guinevere Turner, who was raised in the Lyman Family, widely regarded as a cult, under the influence of charismatic leader Mel Lyman. The Lyman Family included over 100 members who fervently accepted a range of extreme conspiracy theories while rejecting modern media and science (Felton 1973). Upon reflection, Turner opted to leave, wanting to distance herself from what she began to recognize as the cult's misogynistic practices.

We need not speculate about Turner's psychology when making the decision to leave to appreciate that it is not only possible but, presumably, likely that there have been some historical cases of individuals who (in short) have gained vices (either moral or epistemic) in light of exposure to vicious influences but who have, nonetheless, tried to be other than as they are. But if this rather weak point is granted, then—as the proponent of Counterreply 1 might continue—it is false that vices are essentially blameworthy. And if it is false that vices are essentially blameworthy, then we can't (in dismissing the individual reductive virtue/vice model) reason from the fact that agents who polarize are prima facie blameless to the conclusion that it is implausible that they are individually vicious.

The previous reasoning, even though it offers a way of defending a (highly restricted) rejection of the claim that vices are blameworthy, does not succeed in actually militating against the blamelessness objection to the reductive virtue/vice view. This is, to be clear, because the previous reasoning is compatible with there being a presumptive case—at least, to be made from within the Williamson model—for thinking that vices *are* blameworthy, even if rarely they are not.

Even more, though, there is another deeper reason for thinking that if agents who polarize really are blameless for doing so when such polarization is epistemically inappropriate, then we should reject that they are vicious. This deeper reason takes us beyond the Williamson-style model for thinking about blame and blamelessness in terms of primary and derivative norm violation and compliance and into a distinction between kinds of blame that have been defended most influentially by Gary Watson (1996) between *attributivity blame* and *accountability blame*. Roughly, this distinction says that blameworthy conduct is attributable to an agent if it is expressive of who she is. Accountability blameworthiness is different; blameworthy conduct is such that one is accountable for that conduct only if one has had a reasonable opportunity to avoid violating the relevant prescriptive norm.[12]

With this distinction in mind, note that vices involve not only certain kinds of motivations but also that these motivations are habituated and are stable features of the individual's character. This stability feature is what is widely taken to distinguish vices from, say, fleeting moods—or occasions where one acts "out of character". As such, the possession and manifestation of vice (understood as such) will almost surely involve attributivity blame, even if some manifestations of vice do not involve accountability blame—e.g., as when circumstances make such behavior out of one's control. If that is right, then from the stipulation that one is, in fact, blameless (along either the attributivity or accountability dimension), it is going to follow that one is not vicious, given that viciousness implies at least attributivity blame even if not accountability blame.

At this juncture in the dialectic, a final move opens up as follows. Perhaps we grant that all viciousness is blameworthy in at least the attributivity sense, and this goes for both vicious disposition possession and occasions of its manifestation. Even so, agents who polarize must surely manifest accountability blameworthiness for their epistemically bad polarization, *even if this behavior is out of character* and thus even if their polarizing does not involve attributivity blameworthiness.

This final move, of course, shifts us from Counterreply 1 over into the territory of Counterreply 2. Counterreply 2 accepts that vices are blameworthy but then maintains that individuals who polarize are blameworthy. If they are, then we can't reason from putative blameless to a lack of viciousness because the original suggestion that individuals who polarize are blameless is, on closer inspection, incorrect.

In thinking about Counterreply 2, it will be helpful to zero in on whether individuals who polarize are accountability blameworthy (as the foregoing line of thought contends) even if they are not attributivity blameworthy. This transposes to a specific question about the behavior involved in epistemically inappropriate polarizing: let us assume for the sake of discussion that polarizing does involve the violation of some kind of epistemic norm (we need not take a stance for the present purposes what it is). Is the violation of that norm accountability blameworthy or accountability blameless? It is accountability blameless if it is *not* the case that polarizing individuals have, in some relevant way, had a reasonable opportunity to *avoid* polarizing in an epistemically inadequate way.

At this point, it will be helpful to contrast individuals who polarize in a group setting with two example cases that come apart vis-à-vis accountability blameworthiness. On the one hand, we have the case of Alvin Goldman's (1988) "benighted cognizer". On the other hand, we have the case of a modern-day conspiracy theorist—call him Cal—who has become radicalized through a combination of Fox News consumption and the nefarious prescriptive analytics of YouTube's recommender system.[13] Let us now consider each case:

BENIGHTED COGNIZER. Ben is a member of an isolated and benighted community. Many of his methods of belief formation have no connection to truth whatsoever, but they are common lore in Ben's community. Let us suppose that Ben wants to know the best time to sow his crops. According to the lore of his community, in order to achieve this, he will first have to sacrifice a goat and bury it in a sacred place. Then he must sit outside his house until it starts to rain and then return to the burial place. If the sun is shining again by the time he will have arrived, it is time to sow the crops. If not, he will have to return home and continue sitting outside his house until the next rainfall. Ben has flawlessly implemented this procedure and has thereby arrived at a belief that it is time to sow the crops.[14]

CAL. Cal lives in an epistemic bubble in the sense that Fox News is the only channel he watches for news about the world; he avoids all other news outlets by choice. When Cal surfs the internet, he does so to watch YouTube videos about his interests, though YouTube's recommender system, set to the "auto-play" default, often leads him to conspiratorial content. Over time, through this diet of Fox News and YouTube, Cal becomes a full-blown conspiracy theorist: he believes the moon landing was a hoax, that the Illuminati have wiretapped his house, and that Obama's birth certificate is a forgery.

What is common to both Ben and Cal is that each has come to cultivate a range of epistemic vices: gullibility, dogmatism, close-mindedness, etc. Moreover, both Ben and Cal's epistemically vicious inferences are attributivity blameworthy in the sense that such viciousness does express their epistemic character. When Ben draws a bizarre inference about the way crops are influenced and when Cal draws a bizarre inference about the agency of the Illuminati, neither is acting out of character in the slightest.

Where they differ, we want to now suggest, concerns their respective *accountability* blameworthiness. Ben, our benighted cognizer, plausibly lacks the opportunity to have avoided violating the epistemic norms he violates. His situation is, after all, very unusual. He is effectively cut off from the kinds of considerations (e.g., scientific arguments against superstition) that might serve as defeaters for his own style of reasoning. To put this in the language of Ian Hacking (1982), it might well be that Ben cannot, from within his own style of thinking, be reasonably expected even to entertain such defeaters (e.g., scientific rejection of superstition) *as* defeaters, were he to initially come across them. But even if this Hacking-style gloss on the situation is too strong, it remains that Ben is effectively doing what a rational person would attempt to do if embedded in such an epistemically unfortunate situation. It is really not as though he could, isolated implausibly in this way, be expected to easily avoid violating the epistemic norms he is violating.

Cal, by contrast, is in a very different situation. Unlike Ben, who is disconnected from alternative sources of information, Cal is in a kind of self-imposed epistemic bubble. He is exposed to only one kind of news source (Fox News) through his own choosing. And, moreover, although he is led through no obvious fault of his own (via YouTube) to conspiracy theories, he is free to reject the auto-play function. To put it another way, it is entirely within his control to do so. He is a victim of nudging, not of coercion. Cal is, accordingly, accountability blameworthy for violating the epistemic norms he comes to violate and for developing the character he does.

Are those who polarize in an epistemically improper way more like Cal or like Ben, with respect to the accountability they have for violating the epistemic norms they violate? One might be inclined, initially, to deny that bad polarizers are anything like Ben and to suppose then that they must be more akin to Cal and thus be accountability blameworthy in a way that is relevantly analogous to how he is as opposed to lacking such accountability in a way that is relevantly analogous to how Ben does.

However, we think this would be a mistake. Although the details of the benighted cognizer case (as initially proposed by Goldman) are far removed from situations we would ordinarily encounter, and the Cal case much more familiar, the situation of one who polarizes in a group setting is in fact much more akin vis-à-vis accountability to Ben than Cal. A central reason here concerns the control one has to the evidence one is exposed to and how one is exposed to it. Cal has *total* control. Ben has no control, and, to a large extent, neither does the individual-level polarizer. In the kind of deliberative contexts that are germane to polarization, individuals have control over what kind of evidence they share and therefore over what kind of evidence they expose others to—namely they need to decide whether to share their private evidence or to keep it for themselves. However, once group discussion ensues, an evidential Pandora's box opens up: others start sharing their evidence, and as a result, no individual could easily avoid encountering the preponderance of evidence that they encounter that affirms the position toward which they previously leaned. It is not as though the context is one of free, unencumbered inquiry (such as Cal's), whereby the individual who polarizes selects to be exposed to the position-supporting evidence they are exposed to—or could for that matter simply "shut off" exposure to further such evidence by altering the auto-play function on YouTube videos, as Cal freely neglects to do. In typical cases of group polarization, the voices of fellow group members cannot be shut off, at least not as easily as doing a click.

But once these points are made salient, the prospects for arguing that individuals who polarize are accountability blameworthy look rather improbable. And that they do militates against the strongest kind of line that a proponent of Counterreply 2 might press—i.e., one that maintains that individual polarizers, even if not attributivity blameworthy, are at least accountability blameworthy in the way they polarize.

5.2.3 The Problem of Mandevillian Intelligence

A final—and more abstract—problem for the reductive virtue/vice model is what we call, following Paul Smart (2018), the problem of *Mandevillian intelligence*.[15] This problem targets, in particular, the summativist, weakly reductionist component of the model insofar as it involves a reduction of epistemically improper group polarization to a summation of negatively valenced individual dispositions. Cases of Mandevillian intelligence, in short, indicate that such a reduction is problematic in principle because cognitive and epistemic properties that are typically seen as vices at the individual level can—and reasonably often enough do—lead to epistemically desirable dispositions or virtues at the collective level.

This might seem, initially, like a baffling idea. Common sense would suggest that bad character at the individual level (epistemic or otherwise) would simply "transmit" over to the group level.[16] So how can epistemic vice generate epistemic virtue?

One way Smart helps to demystify this phenomenon is to draw an analogy between Mandevillian intelligence and a (roughly) analogous conversion of "vice to virtue" at the individual level—viz., what is called "Inner crowd wisdom" (Hourihan & Benjamin 2010). The inner crowd wisdom phenomenon (a twist on the well-known Wisdom of the Crowd) involves aggregating a series of an individual's judgments to form a "collective" judgment. As a study by Hourihan and Benjamin (2010) has shown, forgetful individuals ended up generating (through a series of their own aggregated individual judgments) more accurate collective judgments than did more attentive individuals with reliable recall. As Smart puts it, "[a]ll that the concept of Mandevillian intelligence seeks to do is to extend this sort of idea to the realms of collective (as opposed to individual) performance" (Smart 2018: 4174).

Let us now consider some concrete examples.

- *Extremism and ignorance.* Zollman (2010) has shown that individual-level "extreme" thinking, as well as individual-level ignorance, are both factors that—so long as they are not combined (*ibid.* 2010: 33)—can contribute fruitfully to truth-conducive group-level cognitive diversity.
- *Impure motivations.* Weisberg and Muldoon (2009) have suggested, in the case of scientific research teams, that impure (i.e., non-epistemic) motivations at the individual level that are indicative of individual-level vice can potentially be valuable at the group level by serving the important function of leading to scientifically novel discoveries that would be unlikely conditioned upon a homogeneity of epistemically oriented motivations (Thagard 1993).
- *Distrust.* According to Smart et al. (2010), distrust (even if epistemically unwarranted) at the individual level between members of a group can lead to collective benefits.
- *Irrational thinking.* Xu et al. (2016) argue that individual-level irrationality can help promote group-level knowledge acquisition in collective search-based tasks.

This list is only a representative sample of extant arguments for Mandevillian intelligence,[17] and we lack the space here to discuss them all. But we need not do so to appreciate how a presumptive argument against the reductive virtue/vice view might proceed. The argument begins with the premise that cognitive shortcomings that (at the individual level at least) obstruct knowledge acquisition, with no uncommon regularity, have been shown to generate collective-level epistemic benefits across a range of collective inquiry tasks. Accordingly, from the bare fact that an individual-level trait is a vice, it is unclear whether we should expect it to *facilitate* or hinder the intellectual aims of a collective of which the individual with that trait participates. As such, unless we have a specific case for thinking that some particular individual-level vice type (or particular individuals-level vice types) in fact best accounts for the tendency of a group to polarize in an epistemically problematic manner, the presumption that what would do so is some vice or another is a non-starter.

At this juncture, the proponent of the reductive virtue/vice view might (as we considered previously) draw attention to the vice of intellectual arrogance as the leading candidate explainer, given the characteristic effects it is claimed to have on discourse. As Alessandra Tanesini (2018) characterizes these effects:

> Arrogance in debate may take many different forms. Arrogant speakers often do not respect the implicit rules of turn-taking. They are prone to interrupting others when they speak. They may also speak at length and deprive others of the same opportunity. In addition, arrogant speakers do not like to be challenged. They respond with anger to genuine questions. They do not answer to objections; instead, they dismiss them without the consideration that they are due.
>
> (2018: 3)

Let us assume that all of these very plausible points are correct. The problem is that there is significant *overlap* between the effects of individual-level arrogance that we are granting and the well-documented effects of individual-level dogmatism. For example, just as arrogant individuals are unwilling to seriously engage the viewpoints of others (e.g., by interrupting them and talking over them), the same holds of dogmatism. In fact, a refusal to give a fair hearing to the opposing side is the central characteristic of dogmatism (Battaly 2018). Likewise, just as, according to Tanesini, arrogant individuals dismiss challenges to their own view, so are dogmatic individuals inclined, as opposed to taking such challenges seriously. But since dogmatic individual-level tendencies (in example cases of Manedevillian intelligence, e.g., Zollman 2010; Smart 2018) have been shown to have effects that run entirely *counter* to epistemically bad polarization—viz., dogmatism at the individual level has been shown to contribute fruitfully to group-level accuracy—the reductive virtue/vice model is not well-positioned to stake its case on arrogance. Put another way: to the extent that arrogance and dogmatism are such that their effects overlap, the fact that dogmatism can lead to group-level epistemic benefits is in tension with the suggestion that what best explains epistemically bad polarization is a vice (arrogance) with such extensive overlap with dogmatism.[18]

In sum, we have shown in this chapter that the reductive virtue/vice model runs up against three substantial worries: what we have called the *pessimism problem*, the *individual blamelessness problem*, and the

Mandevillian intelligence problem. We have considered how the proponent of the view might respond to each objection, and the envisaged responses in each case ran into further problems. The conjunction of these three problems, together with our initial objection to a reliabilist interpretation of the reductive virtue/vice model, offers a presumptive case for thinking that this model should be rejected.

Notes

1. One sophisticated account of epistemic competence is due to Sosa (2015); a minimal conception of an epistemic competence is just a reliable disposition to believe truly when in appropriate shape and situation to do so.
2. See §8.2.3 for further discussion on why the kinds of goals these competences aim to meet—and not others—are relevant.
3. For a different explanation at the individual level, see Bruder et al. (2013). Perhaps unsurprisingly, as Sunstein (2016: 23) remarks, "the best predictor of whether people will accept a conspiracy theory appears to be whether they accept other conspiracy theories".
4. In recent work on the epistemology of conspiracy theories by Quassim Cassam (2015), additional candidate individual level-vices noted as conducive to conspiratorial thinking include, along with Coady's "paranoia" and "naivety", also a combination of gullibility and closed-mindedness.
5. Cassam takes the "get in the way of knowledge" locution to be in line with the way Medina (2013) has used this locution to think about vice.
6. See Tanesini (2016).
7. Arvan (2019) has recently defended what would appear to be a variation of the reductive virtue/vice view for moral polarization specifically. His position is that moral polarization is partly the result of an individual-level meta-ethical (and epistemological) vice of sorts, which is the common belief that moral truths are discovered rather than socially negotiated (viz., what Arvan calls the "Discovery Model" of morality). Arvan then argues that moral and political polarization are likely to be significantly mitigated if larger numbers of individuals (and by extension the groups they compose) overcome this epistemic vice, reconceptualizing moral truths as things to negotiate. Although Arvan's is only an analysis of one type of group polarization ("moral polarization"), it is worth registering that this position type—even if it were generalized beyond cases of moral polarization—would not qualify as a genuine instance of the reductive virtue/vice view. This is because antecedent acceptance of a moral realist position (or realist positions more generally, were the view to be extended) does not align with the profile of an epistemic vice. For one thing, it is certainly not clear that the kind of realism that is implied by the Discovery Model is false in morality; moral realism is among the range of popular options in mainstream metaethics. But, moreover, even if moral realism were false (and thus, even if we grant that prior acceptance of the Discovery Model constitutes a false individual-level starting point), it remains that a large swathe of issues featured in group polarization are matters of fact such that the contested truths are not at all plausibly constructed via negotiation (global warming, client innocence or guilt, the health of the economy, the costs versus benefits of fracking, etc.). For this reason, it is hard to see how realist commitments more generally along the line of what Arvan is calling the Discovery Model would constitute (or even contribute to) individual-level vices at all across a wide range of topics on which groups

tend to polarize. Thanks to a referee at Routledge for prompting discussion on this point.

8. For related discussion of this idea, see Egan (2008).
9. For discussion of this cost, see, for example Alfano (2012).
10. Of course, there might also be normative requirements concerning how one chooses to expose oneself to information or evidence, a point that has been made forcefully by (among others) Baehr (2009) and Goldberg (2016, 2017). However, such normative requirements are premised upon a reasonable level of exposure choice, which is often not present in group polarization cases, where exposure is non-voluntary. For related discussion on this point, see Sunstein (2014) on varieties of choice architecture.
11. See, for example, Cassam (2019) and Battaly (2014).
12. For related discussion, see Levy (2005) and Wolf (2019).
13. See Alfano 2018 et al. and Alfano et al. 2020 for discussion of how prescriptive analytics can play a role in self-radicalization.
14. This is a paraphrasing of Simion et al.'s (2016) gloss on Goldman's (1988) case.
15. Smart uses the term "Mandevillian" in connection with the work of the Anglo-Dutch philosopher Bernard Mandeville (1670–1733). Mandeville, in *The Fable of the Bees* wrote about a causal link between individual-level vice and public (collective) benefits.
16. In fact, there is some evidence that bad character at the individual level will, in certain restricted cases, be amplified at the group level. See Hinsz et al. (2008).
17. For additional discussion, see Smart (2016), which is the predecessor paper to Smart (2018).
18. Note that a structurally similar kind of "overlap" diagnosis will apply, *mutatis mutandis*, if we replace "arrogance", on Tanesini's account, with Cassam's example of "intellectual insouciance". The reason is as follows: just as manifestations of individual-level arrogance and dogmatism overlap, where the latter has been shown to contribute to group-level virtue, likewise, features of intellectual insouciance overlap with both impure motivations as well as ignorance, where both of these features—as reported in studies by Zollman (2010; Weisberg and Muldoon (2009)—when manifested at the individual level, can actually promote (as opposed to obstruct) the group's successful convergence on the truth. In short, then, what goes for arrogance also seems to go for insouciance.

6 The Collective Heuristic/ Bias Model

6.1 The View in Outline

Let us consider now the *collective heuristic/bias model*, the view that adequate group polarization is explained in terms of *collective heuristics* and epistemically inadequate group polarization in terms of *collective biases*. According to this picture, group polarization, understood as a collective belief-forming process, is a feature of the group itself, and it is to be identified as a cognitive heuristic of the collective agent (in the good cases) or as a cognitive bias (in the bad cases) rather than as an irreducibly collective virtue or vice. To appreciate this interpretation, it will be helpful to first take as a starting point a familiar case of group cognition— viz., a case of cognition where a group has an epistemic feature that no individual member has. One well-known such example in the literature is given by Edwin Hutchins (1995) and involves a ship crew navigating a ship to port.

As Jennifer Lackey (2014) concisely summarizes the case, which is a reference point in the literature on distributed cognition:

> In such a case, the ship's behavior as it safely travels into the port is clearly well-informed and deliberate, leading to the conclusion that there is collective knowledge present. More precisely, it is said that the crew as a whole knows, for instance, that they are traveling north at 80 miles per hour, or that the ship itself knows this, even though no single crew member does.
>
> (Lackey 2014: 282)[1]

If a group can possess knowledge that no single member of the group possesses—as is the suggestion in Hutchins' case—then perhaps a group can manifest a heuristic or a bias that cannot be explained just as an aggregation of individual heuristics or biases of its members. This, at any rate, is the interpretation of group polarization being advanced on the collective heuristic/bias interpretation.

As we saw in §4.2.3, there are two central approaches to the notions of "heuristic" and "bias". On the heuristics-and-biases program (Tversky &

Kahneman 1974), heuristics are conceived as automatic effort-effective mental shortcuts that nevertheless lead to systematic errors, and they are in this way eminently irrational. By contrast, on the fast-and-frugal program (Gigerenzer & Goldstein 1996), heuristics are best conceived as fast mental shortcuts that, in certain conditions of uncertainty, can outperform more complex methods of belief formation or decision making; moreover, using heuristics in such conditions is rational, according to this approach. While both research programs have mainly focused on *individual* heuristics and biases, they have also carried out some research on heuristics and biases *at the collective level*. Unsurprisingly, given the divergent nature of their research agendas, the kind of collective heuristics and biases hypothesized and empirically tested are different.

Despite such a divergence, both conceptions of heuristics and biases need not be incompatible in an *epistemological* account of group deliberation. Indeed, a proponent of the collective heuristic/bias model could argue that if the postulated heuristics and biases are in fact irreducibly collective, then the epistemic appropriateness or inappropriateness of group polarization can be explained in those terms. The generalized reasoning would be as follows. Take the negatively valenced biases of the heuristics-and-biases program and the positively valenced heuristics of the fast-and-frugal approach: just as in some cases of group biases and heuristics individual heuristics and biases (as conceived by the two research programs) are respectively *enhanced* and *exacerbated* in a group setting, so likewise, in some cases of group polarization, individual heuristics and biases are enhanced and exacerbated in a group setting. To the extent that the former fact motivates the suggestion that such group heuristics and biases are collective in ways that go significantly beyond (and, therefore, that cannot be reduced to) the summation of individual heuristics and biases, by parity of reasoning, the latter fact motivates the suggestion that (i) *epistemically adequate* group polarization is the product of a collective heuristic and that (ii) *epistemically inadequate* group polarization is the outcome of a collective bias, both irreducibly so.

Consider the fast-and-frugal program. Although most research in this program has been carried out on individual heuristics, some research on fast-and-frugal *collective heuristics* can potentially help understand how epistemically appropriate group polarization could be the outcome of an irreducibly collective heuristic. By way of illustration, Reimer and Hoffrage (2006) have investigated (via simulations) whether two heuristics involving limited processing of information—namely, the minimalist and the take-the-best heuristics—lead to more accurate outcomes *in group settings* than more exhaustive information-processing strategies. The reported results differ (in favor of either the limited or the exhaustive strategies) depending on the informational conditions within the group, especially when the quality of the information available to group members varies.[2] In the same vein, as discussed in Chapter 3, the epistemic appropriateness of group polarization depends, among other things, on the quality of the information available to group members. Given this similarity, it is not inconceivable that the epistemic appropriateness of group polarization might be grounded in the fact that an irreducibly collective heuristic is capable of achieving accurate outcomes in the kind of group settings that are typical of good cases of polarization.

Concerning *epistemically inappropriate* group polarization, the most plausible option for the proponent of the collective heuristic/bias model is to understand group polarization as an irreducibly collective *irrational* bias akin to the kind of collective biases postulated—and empirically tested—by social psychologists following the heuristics-and-biases research agenda. In this research program, several of the cognitive biases discovered in individuals have also been found in group settings. There is evidence, for instance, that hindsight bias (perceiving past events as such that one knew, all along, that they would have occurred), the representativeness heuristic (which makes people think that an event is likely because it is similar or representative of some category), or confirmation bias (searching, recalling, or interpreting information that supports one's preexisting beliefs) also affects groups. As it turns out, some such biases affect groups and individuals to roughly the same extent—as is the case of hindsight bias (Stahlberg et al. 1995)—while others are amplified in groups—as is the case of the representativeness heuristic (Argote et al. 1986) and confirmation bias (Schulz-Hardt et al. 2000).

To better grasp how epistemically bad group polarization can be understood as an irreducibly collective irrational bias of the sort the heuristics-and-biases program postulates, let us consider group confirmation bias in a bit more detail.[3] Group confirmation bias is the description that has been given to a result reported in a series of experiments by Schulz-Hardt et al. (2000), which consistently have shown that the same confirmation bias that has been found for individuals also occurs in groups, so that the more group members had chosen the same alternative prior to the group discussion, the more strongly the group preferred information supporting that alternative (2000: 666). In other words, homogeneous groups are more liable to group confirmation bias than heterogeneous groups. Furthermore, Schulz-Hardt and colleagues reported experiments that indicate that the tendency to gather data that confirmed their original position is a bias that individuals exhibit *to a greater extent* when in a group setting than outside a group. This is indicative that group bias is an irreducibly collective bias. As Schulz-Hardt and colleagues put it:

> If the differences between homogeneous and heterogeneous groups were a pure aggregation phenomenon, then the only significant effects should be a main effect for information (supporting [information] should be preferred to conflicting ones) and a two-way interaction between information and group composition. . . . On the contrary,

if the differences between homogeneous and heterogeneous groups were a group-level phenomenon, then two additional effects should emerge. First, real groups should request fewer [information] than statisticized groups. Second, and even more importantly . . . [h]omogeneous groups should be more biased than expected on the basis of their statisticized baselines, while heterogeneous groups should be less biased compared to that baseline. All in all, the differences between homogeneous and heterogeneous groups should be more pronounced than predicted by a statistical combination of individual information requests.

(Schulz-Hardt et al. 2000: 662)

In light of this, the defender of the collective heuristic/bias model of group polarization would follow Schulz-Hardt and colleagues in thinking that a bias that is *magnified* by a collective cannot simply be a summation of the individual biases of its members. The idea, then, would be to draw an analogy with the kind of irrational biases that affect groups more than individuals—e.g., the representativeness heuristic, confirmation bias—and argue that biases of that sort produce epistemically inappropriate group polarization. The difference with such biases would be, of course, in the effect produced. For example, while group confirmation bias makes groups exhibit a tendency to search for supporting information, the kind of irrational tendency exhibited by groups undergoing the "group polarization bias" would be to form an epistemically inappropriate, more extreme opinion than prior to deliberation. In both cases, at any rate, the relevant group biases would be irreducibly collective.

6.2 Problems

As we will see next, the previous interpretation of the collective bias model does not hold up in light of the following two problems: the *empirical adequacy problem* and the *type-1/type-2 problem*. Let us take these in order.

6.2.1 The Empirical Adequacy Problem

The first problem, concerning epistemically inadequate group polarization, can be briefly stated as follows. Unlike the notion of epistemic vice, which is neither used nor originates in psychology, the notion of cognitive bias is both widely used and stems from research in psychology. This means that the extension of the term "cognitive bias" is fixed by psychologists—whereas the extension of the term "epistemic vice" is fixed by philosophers. The immediate consequence of this is that we should trust psychologists in calling "biases" the phenomena that they referred to as such. In this sense, group polarization and group biases are considered clearly different phenomena in the psychological literature, which means that unless a relationship is established between them theoretically and, especially, empirically, the collective bias model remains an empirically inadequate interpretation of the metaphysics and epistemology of group polarization.

Concerning epistemically adequate group polarization, independently of the results reported by Reimer and Hoffrage—i.e., even if they predicted a group polarization effect when heuristics are used within a group—there is a powerful reason not to use the fact that groups can implement fast-and-frugal heuristics to infer, by parity of reasoning, that group polarization, in the good cases, is produced by a kind of *irreducibly collective* fast-and-frugal heuristic (albeit, perhaps, a different one from the ones tested by Reimer and Hoffrage). That is, even if we assume that a group can in principle instantiate an epistemic property (a fast-and-frugal heuristic) that cannot be explained in terms of a summation of related epistemic properties of group members (as in cases of distributed cognition), this assumption cannot have as rationale Reimer and Hoffrage's model. The reason is simple: in their simulations, Reimer and Hoffrage tested how "group performance is affected by the decision strategies that are used by *individual* group members" (2006: 406), where the relevant group decision is determined, in turn, by *aggregating* the individuals' decisions by means of a majority rule. In other words, the seemingly non-reductionist assumption that group polarization is a kind of fast-and-frugal heuristic cannot be defended on the basis of facts reported about aggregations of individual heuristics in a group setting. This is thus a thoroughly *summativist* and therefore *reductionist account of group polarization* and so not a genuine candidate for an irreducibly collective epistemic heuristic.

6.2.2 The Type-1/Type-2 Problem

The phenomenon reported by Schulz-Hardt and colleagues under the description of group confirmation bias might still be a bona fide collective cognitive bias. *Even if* that is the case, there is a further and more general problem waiting in the wings, which renders it problematic to suppose that group polarization, in particular, could be a collective epistemic *bias*. The problem in short concerns the dynamics of deliberation apposite to group polarization in paradigmatic cases. Even if we suppose the subject of the deliberation is the group itself—viz., the group engaging in internal deliberation—such deliberation would nonetheless plausibly involve, in the main, type-2 thinking characterized by the adducing and evaluating of reasons and arguments. Biases, however, are distinguished partly as a function of type-1 processing (cf., Mercier & Sperber 2017), a point that has been influentially stressed by (among others) Kahneman (passim) in his work on cognitive bias at the individual level. Thus, we submit, features distinctive of group polarization render it such that, at the collective level at least, it is not plausibly produced by—and hence construed as—a genuine group-level cognitive bias.

Is there scope for a proponent of the collective heuristic/bias model to press back against this objection? We will consider two strategies of counterreply. The first strategy draws attention to the following: that rational deliberation characteristic of type-2 processing is itself uncontroversially *susceptible* to biases. After all, individual-level deliberation is often biased in various well-reported ways despite the fact that deliberation *itself* primarily involves type-2 thinking. But then, as this line of thought would go, the rationale for dismissing the collective heuristic/ bias model is vitiated.

The previous line of reply is, we submit, misguided. What is problematic for a proponent of the collective heuristic/bias model is that biases do not *depend* on rational deliberation, even though deliberation is susceptible to biased thinking. It is this point that the collective heuristic/bias model gets intractably wrong.

However, even if the previous line of thinking does little to defuse the Type-1/Type-2 problem, there is a more sophisticated style of reply that is available to the proponent of the collective heuristic/bias model, and we will focus our attention on it. This more sophisticated style of counterreply—a kind of argument from disanalogy—attempts to cleave a wedge between (i) the kind of features that are distinctive of cognitive biases at the individual level and (ii) the kind of features that distinguish cognitive biases at the collective level and maintain that the former kinds of features need not be expected to match the latter in all respects but only some.

The "disanalogy" counterreply begins by pointing out a kind of argument pattern that collective epistemologists—and researchers of collective intentionality more generally—will object to. The argument pattern says: if state S, when realized at the individual level, has property P, then a collective variant of state S, S^*, has P. Consider, for example, the state of belief. If we substitute "belief" for S and "non-voluntariness" for P, the previous argument pattern tells us that collective belief should have the property of being non-voluntary given that individual belief has the property of being non-voluntary. However, on almost all extant accounts of group belief that are non-summativist (e.g., Gilbert 1987, 2013; Tuomela 1992; Tollefsen 2015), group beliefs are conceived of in such a way that the kind of non-voluntariness we find at the individual level will not hold. Think, in particular, of joint commitment accounts: on such accounts it is (voluntary) individual-level agreements to behave in certain ways that ground the group belief.

This point has an important ramification for the Type-1/Type-2 objection. The ramification is that, to the extent that the objection maintains that group-level biases should have the features of individual-level biases, this must not be *because* it is implied by the previous invalid reasoning pattern. Rather, it would need to be shown that there is something particular about bias such that the kind of thinking that characterizes it at the individual will also be the kind of thinking that characterizes it (or at least, often enough characterizes it) at the collective level. Put another way, without a particular reason to think that biases cannot simply consist in patterns of (what would be) Type-2 rather than Type-1 thinking at the collective level, the Type-1/Type-2 objection against the collective heuristic/bias view is undercut.

This counterreply makes an important point, one that we grant. There is no a priori entailment between the features of individual state properties and their collective counterparts. This is why, in cases like the individual state of belief, the possibility that collective manifestations of belief are going to differ along the voluntariness dimension from their individual manifestations is not something that should be foreclosed as a matter of any kind of principle. The same arguably, goes (albeit, somewhat trivially) for the property of privileged access. It is a hallmark of almost all individual-level intentional attitudes, including emotions, that they enjoy privileged access, which is to say that they are available only to a single subject to know about via introspection. In the case of collective attitudes, there is no reason to expect that they would have this same kind of epistemic property that characterizes our individual-level mental states.

That said, we think the proponent of the Type-1/Type-2 objection to the collective heuristic/bias model has a response to make here. The response begins with a distinction: even though it is false that if state *S*, when realized at the individual level, has property *P*, then a collective variant of state *S*, *S**, has *P;* it is *likewise* false that if state *S*, when realized at the individual level, has property *P*, then *this is not evidence that* a collective variant of state *S*, *S**, has *P*. That this latter principle is false is *especially the case* when the individual-level state's having *P* is essential to making that state the kind of state that it is.

To appreciate the previous point, let us stick with the example of individual and collective beliefs and their properties. A widely held view in the literature on the normativity of belief maintains that beliefs aim at truth, in the sense that: for an individual, *S* and belief *B*, *S*'s belief that *B* is correct only if *B* is true. Beliefs that are not true miss their mark, and they are defective for doing so even if they are, e.g., held on the basis of good reasons.

Being correct if true is plausibly a necessary condition for an attitude's being a belief (even if it is not a sufficient condition).[4] This should not be surprising when one considers that beliefs are cognitive or theoretical (as opposed to practical) intentional attitudes with a mind-to-world direction of fit (Anscombe 1957; Humberstone 1992; Williamson 2017).

The idea here is that the realization (i.e., success) for a cognitive (or theoretical) intentional mental state involves fitting mind-to-world, whereas, the realization for a practical mental state (e.g., desire, intention, etc.) involves fitting world-to-mind (Frost 2014).

If a collective-level attitude had a *practical* direction of fit (e.g., as is the case with a collective intention), that is evidence that that collective attitude is not a belief. Such an attitude's correctness would depend on whether the world is changed to match the attitude's content, not the other way around. We should, as it were, *expect* that collective beliefs, *qua* beliefs, will have a mind-to-world direction of fit. If a collective attitude has a *world-to-mind* direction of fit, then this is evidence that the attitude in question is simply not a belief. In this way, the property of having a mind-to-world direction of fit is best understood as an essential property of an attitude's being a belief (something that must "carry over" to the collective level), whereas property of being "non-voluntary" is, by contrast, better understood as a property that beliefs have at the individual level—but just on account of the kind of cognitive vehicles that are the material realizers of beliefs at the individual level. If beliefs are realized at the collective level, they of course need not have these same material realizers and, accordingly, need not additionally have these properties.

With this in mind, the key question, vis-à-vis the prospects of the disanalogy counterreply we are canvassing vis-à-vis the Type-1/Type-2 objection, is: *which* properties of a bias, when realized at the individual level, are essential to something's being a bias (in a way that, by parity of reasoning, corresponds with how having a mind-to-world direction of fit is essential to an attitude's being a belief? By contrast, which properties of individual-level biases are inessential—viz., which are more akin to the non-voluntariness and privileged access properties of individual beliefs, which need not be expected to carry over to the collective level (even if they might do so)?

At this point, we want to suggest that, to the extent that biases at the individual level have the property of corresponding with Type-1 rather than Type-2 thinking, this is best understood as an essential rather than expendable property of a bias and, as such, is the kind of property that we really *should* expect any bona fide bias to retain if is to be a collective property of a group. Here is the argument: if a bias *lacked* the property of corresponding with Type-1 thinking, then a bias would not be distinct in kind from any other general sort of rational mistake. But biases constitute a *distinctive* category of rational mistakes: this is a point that is uncontroversially accepted, including by those who disagree about how biases are cognitively realized (see §5.2.1 for discussion). We should, accordingly, expect that if something is a genuine "bias" at the collective level, it will correspond with Type-1 thinking. And so, if group polarization is a bias, this is what we should expect.

But, as this reasoning continues, this warranted expectation is simply not borne out. Group polarization, in short, is produced and sustained through Type-2 thinking—consider, for example, the evidence from persuasive arguments theory as a representative point. It is accordingly not going to be viable to defend the view that epistemically inappropriate group polarization is best explained in terms of a collective bias while at the same time maintaining that it is a bias that consists in Type-2 rather than Type-1 thinking.

Is the proponent of the collective heuristic/bias view, at this juncture, out of moves? Not quite. There remains the option of granting that there is necessarily a tight relationship between bias (as such) and Type-1 thinking (at either the individual or collective level) and then to simply insist that paradigmatic cases of group polarization are ones where group is best interpreted as doing exactly this (despite initial indications to the contrary).

To see how such a move might be fleshed out, consider as a reference point a study by Bail et al. (2018) involving U.S. Democrats and Republicans on Twitter. The Democrats were exposed to a conservative Twitter bot and the Republicans to a Liberal Twitter bot. The result of this exposure was that the Republicans expressed significantly more conservative viewpoints after exposure to the liberal Twitter bot, and the Democrats' attitudes became slightly more liberal (though not significantly so) following exposure to the Conservative Twitter bot.

If we focus in on the Republican case, it might look as though we have, prima facie, an example of a group that both polarizes and does so "unthinkingly"—viz., not on the basis of any kind of exposure to arguments for their viewpoints but simply as a kind of unthinking reaction to exposure to viewpoints of the other side.

Moving in this direction, though, quickly becomes a kind of "double-edged" sword for a proponent of the collective heuristic/bias view. The reason is that the kind of evidence we find in studies like Bail's would seem to support, if anything, the reductive heuristic/bias view rather than a collective heuristic/bias view. This is because the Republicans' tendency to move toward more extreme positions (after exposure to a liberal Twitter bot) is one that can be explained apart from any interactions they have with other similar thinking members of their group—and entirely in terms of their interaction with outgroup members—in keeping with self-categorization theory.

Thus, it looks as though, if there is going to be a successful account of the metaphysics and epistemology of group polarization framed in terms of heuristics and biases, it will be the reductive rather than collective model:

The Reductive Heuristic/Bias Model: group polarization as a summation of individual heuristics or biases.

The reductive heuristic/bias model—which we will evaluate in the next chapter—is one of our two remaining accounts. The other, the collective virtue/vice model, holds:

> **The Collective Virtue/Vice Model**: group polarization as an irreducibly collective epistemic virtue or vice.

Each of these positions is at least prima facie plausible. Neither at any rate can be dismissed out of hand. In order to assess the comparative merits, it will be important to look at them more closely, filling out some further details and thinking about these details in the context of the features and causes of group polarization outlined in Chapter 2, as well as in terms of the epistemology of group polarization as laid out in Chapter 3.

Notes

1. See also Bird (2014) for another notable articulation of this kind of view.
2. Reimer and Katsikopoulos (2004) have also investigated how the use of the recognition heuristic among group members affects group performance.
3. See Klayman (1995) and Nickerson (1998) for two reviews of confirmation bias and its varieties.
4. Cases of guessing, for example, cast doubt on the sufficiency of having truth as a standard of correctness for an attitude's being a belief.

7 The Reductive Heuristic/ Bias Model

7.1 The View in Outline

The reductive heuristic/bias model is the view according to which epistemically appropriate and inappropriate group polarization is best theorized as a summation of, respectively, individual heuristics and biases. A first point to note is that "*group* polarization" is a term that proponents of this model will object to as potentially misleading. After all, on this proposal, polarization is modeled not as the outcome of an irreducibly collective group process but as the result of aggregating the outputs of individual belief-forming processes of its members, namely certain heuristics and biases.[1] Thus, for each individual, the individual can be said so succumb to (something like) the *magnification-of-previously-held-view-after-deliberating-in-a-group-setting heuristic/bias* or, perhaps, other more basic heuristics or biases that combine to generate this complex heuristic/bias. And "group polarization" is just a name for the aggregate that results from such individual-level heuristics and biases.

On the reductive heuristic/bias model, the *causes* of group polarization must be explicable in terms of individual biases and their associated heuristics, and a prima facie desideratum of an explanation of such causes is that the explanation can be potentially reconciled with persuasive argument theory, social comparison theory, and self-categorization theory.[2]

Persuasive arguments theory, given a reductive heuristic/bias model spin, will thus say that the causes of group polarization are individuals applying the kind of heuristics and biases the following of which generate polarized beliefs, such as a more extreme version of the belief the individual began with prior to engaging in deliberation. We can find candidate heuristics and biases both in the fast-and-frugal and the heuristics-and-biases research programs.

Consider the *fast-and-frugal research program* first. Recall that, as per this approach, it is sometimes rational to rely on individual-level heuristics as long as doing so tends to lead to epistemically optimal results under certain conditions. In this way, some of the "fast-and-frugal" heuristics investigated in this research program can potentially explain how groups might polarize in epistemically appropriate ways. Consider, by way of illustration, a case of (seemingly) epistemically unproblematic group polarization such that all group members individually implement the *take-the-best heuristic* based on limited information—the way the take-the-best heuristic works is to first try the cue (e.g., the information) with the highest validity ignoring the rest (Gigerenzer & Goldstein 1996).

> HEURISTICAL DELIBERATION. A medical team needs to treat a patient suffering from disease Y. All team members individually *suspect* that treatment X cures such a disease and meet to discuss whether this is the case. All individually possess good, albeit limited evidence supporting the proposition that X cures Y. For example, each knows of one randomized clinical trial (a different one in each case) that confirms the suspected hypothesis. During group discussion, all group members share their evidence but do it, first, with the person to their right and then with the rest. Interestingly, all team members implement the take-the-best heuristic to form their individual beliefs about the discussed issue, with the following implication: when a given group member is exposed to the information offered by the person to her left, since this information always stems from the results of a randomized clinical trial (given the group's initial evidential setup), she regards the information received as having high validity, ignoring any further evidence she might be exposed to during group discussion. By implementing the take-the-best heuristic in this way, all group members move from suspecting to believing that X cures Y and do it solely based on good reasons, albeit limited ones, given the group's pool of evidence. The upshot is that the pre-discussion group's average with respect to the discussed proposition increases, i.e., the group polarizes.

Arguably, the medical team polarizes in a way that we might describe as epistemically adequate. If this is not initially obvious, just consider our argument in Chapter 3 that group polarization can be epistemically appropriate when group members draw only on limited good evidence, a point that was illustrated by the NOT-SO-GOOD SCIENTISTS case. To the extent that our assessment of that case is on the right track, then appealing to individual heuristics such as the take-the-best heuristic is one way in which the proponent of the reductive heuristic/bias model could account for good cases of group polarization.

What about epistemically problematic group polarization? Here the proponent of the reductive heuristic/bias model could appeal to the kind of cognitive biases postulated by the *heuristics-and-biases research program*. One candidate bias that could generate polarized group beliefs in the kind of group settings described by persuasive arguments theory is *confirmation bias*. For instance, the proponent of the reductive heuristic/bias model might argue that when a large number of group members tend to share the same kinds of views and most fall prey to confirmation bias, discussions within the group will tend to be dominated by information that already supports the view held by most of them, which results in a polarized group belief. This kind of phenomenon is reported, e.g., in online group polarization (Del Vicario et al. 2016, 2017).

The epistemic significance of confirmation bias in polarized groups—those which, let us suppose, only polarize due to informational influences, as per persuasive arguments theory—is revealed by the fact that it does evidential filtering work in a particular direction: it filters out, from group discussion, any potentially relevant evidence that counts against the dominant view within the group. As we argued in Chapter 3, not considering potentially relevant counterevidence—at least when there is an epistemic obligation to do so—is a reason for considering group polarization epistemically inappropriate. Thus, on the reductive heuristic/bias model—when spelled out in terms of an aggregation of individual confirmation biases being manifested—most cases of group polarization are plausibly expected to be like this, i.e., epistemically problematic. In fact, according to Mercier (2011), individual confirmation bias can lead to polarization even—and perhaps notably—in groups of like-minded experts, who "tap into their vast knowledge to defend whatever opinion they hold" (Mercier 2011: 313).

Interestingly, this does not mean that individual confirmation bias cannot *at least in principle* give rise to epistemically appropriate group polarization. The conditions under which this is possible—within the reductive heuristic/bias framework—are such that *all* the evidence available bearing on the dominant group view would need to be good supporting evidence, and further there would have to be no obligation to consider good counterevidence during group discussion (because such counterevidence does not exist). If the rest of epistemic factors (as laid out in Chapter 3) are adequate, group polarization in such particular conditions *might* be epistemically appropriate.

If this is not obvious, just consider an example of a group whose members are competent scientists who believe that Earth is an oblate spheroid and hence that it is not flat. Even if they all individually fall prey to strong confirmation bias (in line with Mercier's remarks), the evidential filtering work that such individual biases do might still be epistemically appropriate if there is no good evidence available against the group's dominant view: that Earth is not flat. As a matter of fact, there is no good evidence against it. Be that as it may, we leave for the proponent of the reductive heuristic/bias model to determine whether cases of this sort count as cases of epistemically appropriate group polarization or else whether they are problematic. Our intention here has been merely to show that it is in principle possible to account for epistemically *adequate* group polarization in terms of individual cognitive biases such as the well-known confirmation bias.

So far, we have considered how the reductive heuristic/bias model could be spelled out in terms of individual heuristics and biases related to *information acquisition and distribution*, i.e., assuming that group polarization is a purely informational phenomenon, as per persuasive arguments theory. But the model is also compatible with the other two main psychological theories of group polarization. For instance, *social comparison theory*, given a reductive heuristic/bias model spin, will say that individuals exhibit at least two kinds of heuristics and associated biases in group settings. First, after estimating the group average concerning an opinion, they perceive themselves as more extreme than the estimated average, which results in a biased underestimation of the real group average. Next, during collective deliberation, and as a result of the social comparison process noted, individuals then present themselves as more extreme than the initial group average (the consequent belief being a biased belief), a consequence of which is a distorted group norm that appears to legitimize extreme positions. Given that this explanation of group polarization primarily appeals to non-epistemic factors, what is explained then is how group polarization can go epistemically wrong (cf. Chapter 3).

Self-categorization theory also explains group polarization in terms of non-epistemic factors and, in particular, in terms of ingroup/outgroup salience. This could be accommodated on the reductive heuristic/bias model by simply noting that group members are individually biased toward accepting ingroup norms and toward rejecting outgroup positions, which would explain why in epistemically problematic cases of group polarization intragroup differences are minimized and intergroup differences maximized.

On the reductive heuristic/bias model, then, the epistemic appropriateness and inappropriateness of the phenomenon itself are explicable primarily in terms of individual-level heuristics and biases in broadly the manner just suggested.

7.2 Problems

We want to now suggest that the reductive heuristic/bias model faces two problems: what we will call the *polarization entrepreneurs problem* and the *irreducibility problem*.

7.2.1 The Polarization Entrepreneurs Problem

According to the *polarization entrepreneurs problem*, some cases of group polarization arise or are intensified because the group contains some individuals who play a role in *intentionally* facilitating the adoption of extreme views within a group, by using various kinds of tactics, including tactics the use of which capitalizes on the polarization entrepreneurs' knowledge of group tendencies and individual weaknesses. A notable example Sunstein gives of polarization entrepreneurs is that of terrorist leaders who impose psychological pressures to accelerate ideological movement in extreme directions, including stifling dissenting views and restricting the argument pools.

As Sunstein (2009) puts it:

> Terrorist leaders act as polarization entrepreneurs. They help to create enclaves of like-minded people. They stifle dissenting views and do not tolerate internal disagreement. They take steps to ensure a high degree of internal solidarity. They restrict the relevant argument pool and take full advantage of reputational forces, above all, by using the incentives of group approval and disapproval. Terrorist acts themselves are motivated by these forces and incentives. In fact, terrorist organizations impose psychological pressures to accelerate the movement in extreme directions. Here group membership plays a key role.
>
> (Sunstein 2009: 116)

More generally, Sunstein defines polarization entrepreneurs as those who "attempt to create communities of like-minded people, and they are aware that these communities will not only harden positions but also move them to a more extreme point" (2009: 34).

If Sunstein is right that polarization entrepreneurs can and oftentimes (in particular in the case of terrorist online use, which he documents) do facilitate group polarization (*ibid.*), then this much counts against a theory of group polarization that explains the epistemology of group polarization in terms of a mere aggregation of individual heuristics and biases. As we've noted, heuristics are generally taken to be, as Kahneman (2011) notes, a form of type-1 as opposed to type-2 processing and as such do not involve *rational planning* of the sort that can be attributed to polarization entrepreneurs. If anything, the polarization entrepreneurs problem reveals an explanatory limitation of the reductive heuristic/bias model.

Polarization entrepreneurs, according to Sunstein, are not *merely* exploiting a phenomenon that is itself accounted for through heuristic or bias. Rather, they are actively driving the process of polarization, through *deliberate planning*. Of course, agents capable of this sort of deliberate planning, e.g., agents with high-level critical skills, can be biased too, even to a greater extent than agents with lower critical skills. For example, Kahan et al. (2017) have found that subjects with greater quantitative-reasoning capacity can more strongly fall prey to motivated reasoning (by selectively conforming their interpretation of the evidence to the result most consistent with their political views). However, as long as it is possible that polarization entrepreneurs are unbiased at any level and perfectly rational at what they are doing, the reductive heuristic/bias model locates the explanation of group polarization at the wrong place, namely at the level of individual heuristics and biases.

The friend of an "individual-level" bias model might, even so, attempt to press back here along the following lines: paradigmatic polarization entrepreneurs are often enough particularly biased in various ways, and their influence on the group discourse, which they use to actively drive the polarization process, involves the spread of biased thinking (via the signaling from their position of influence pro-attitudes about such thinking).[3] Take, for example, the primary proponents of QAnon-sourced conspiracy theories, which have had well-documented polarizing effects on Twitter and other social media (Zuckerman 2019). The relevant entrepreneurs here have a track record of manifesting—and encouraging—racial, economic, social, educational, gender, and other biases. Accordingly, as the rebuttal would go, even if some polarization entrepreneurs are not biased at all, we have a presumptive case for thinking that a good portion of them in actual cases are not only biased themselves but encouraging of such bias through the influence they exercise over the polarizing process (think here of those who spread QAnon posts with a large Twitter following).

However, a further counterreply awaits: even if the previous claim is granted—that is, even if it is simply conceded that polarization entrepreneurs are often enough biased themselves (and indeed, especially so!)—this concession does not imply that we should think that polarization occurs in virtue of this (and other individual-level) biases, as the model under discussion predicts. And, in fact, we have reason to think that exactly the opposite is true. Take again the example of the candidate polarization entrepreneurs most plausibly responsible for initiating and sustaining QAnon conspiracy theories on social media. According to a recent study by Schabes (2020), the "entrepreneurship" of these highly polarizing conspiracies are thoughtfully planned and carefully executed. But that is just to say that these polarization entrepreneurs, even if they themselves manifest many (and even extreme) biases in the positions they hold to be true, they are such that the entrepreneurship of polarization is best understood as associated not with biased thinking but with careful, deliberate Type-2 thinking.

7.2.2 The Irreducibility Problem

According to what we may call the *irreducibility problem*, the reductive heuristic/bias model—by offering an explanation of the epistemic properties of group polarization entirely at the level of an aggregation of properties of individuals (viz., their heuristics and biases)—problematically forecloses the possibility that at least some aspects of group polarization are properties that arise only via the *dynamics* of group member interactions and not merely through any aggregate of individual actions and or/ beliefs.

This point can be made helpfully with reference to dynamical systems theory (DST), which articulates conditions, generally speaking, under which the collaborative behavior of two (or more) individuals gives rise to *irreducibly* collective properties—viz., properties of a system that do not belong to the contributing subsystems.[4] In particular, according to DST, what suffices for such irreducibly collective properties is the existence of nonlinear interactions that arise out of feedback loops between the contributing parts (Clark & Chalmers 1998; Chemero 2009; Froese et al. 2013; Sutton et al. 2010; Theiner & O'Connor 2010; Wegner et al. 1985; Tollefsen & Dale 2011; Palermos 2011, 2014). Take, for example, the case—often noted in the context of DST in cognitive science—of *transactive memory systems*. Transactive Memory Systems (TMSs) (Wegner et al. 1985; Wegner 1986; Wegner 1995; Hollingshead 1998a, 1998b; Hollingshead & Brandon 2003) are groups of two or more individuals who interact and collaboratively encode, store, and retrieve information that neither alone could retrieve without mutually interacting with the other (Palermos 2016: 3). In such cases, the coupled system has cognitive features over and above the aggregate of the individual cognitive systems, because "they think about things in ways they would not alone" (Wegner et al. 1985: 254).[5]

Returning now to group polarization, just as in the case of transactive memory systems, two individuals can give rise to a coupled memory process, one with irreducible properties, as a result of the presence of feedback loops (e.g., Theiner 2010: 381); groups of individuals who interact continuously and reciprocally (on the basis of feedback loops) with each other "have the potential to display *emergent* cognitive properties that no individual member has, or might even be capable of having" (our emphasis).[6] A group's tendency to polarize (on all three psychological accounts) appears to be at least a partial function of continuous mutual interaction (exposure to each other's positions as well as in some cases each other's positions and their arguments), which then leads to responsive behavior that in turn has further effects and responses, which culminate in the group's polarization.

While we think the previous considerations make it very plausible that the epistemology of group polarization should be accounted for in collective terms, rather than in terms of reducible properties of a group, the trouble for the reductive heuristic/bias model does not actually require that we insist on this point. Rather, and more weakly, the problem is that this model *forecloses* the possibility that group polarization is the outcome of an irreducibly collective process of a group (e.g., an interaction dynamic between group members), such as a transactive memory system.

To bring these points into sharp relief, consider cases such as GOOD SCIENTISTS and NOT-SO-GOOD SCIENTISTS in Chapter 3. Such cases show that it is *not* necessarily the case that, if a group polarizes in an epistemically adequate way, this is due to an aggregation of heuristics operative at the individual level. Moreover, such cases are not anecdotal but illustrative examples of how groups of scientists and other researchers polarize in adequate ways.

Likewise, group polarization can be epistemically problematic without any flaw at the individual level. In particular, it is not *necessary* for epistemically inappropriate group polarization that group members manifest individual biases. For example, a third party can prevent a group of deliberators exhibiting no biases (but only epistemic virtues) from accessing good counterevidence they should discuss. In such a situation, the group would polarize if most group members initially lean toward the same view, and the only evidence they draw on during group discussion supports their preferred view. When that happens, the failure of the group to discuss good counterevidence is enough to make the group's polarization epistemically inadequate (as we have argued in Chapter 3) even when group members are individually blameless for such an omission. After all, we can suppose, they are competent both at collecting and evaluating information and certainly do their best on both fronts by competently collecting and evaluating the best evidence available—i.e., evidence that, due to the third party's clever manipulation, supports only the group's pre-discussion view.

In addition, operative biases at the individual level are not *sufficient* for epistemically inadequate group polarization either.[7] Consider the following case:

> BIASED POLITICIANS. A group of biased and like-minded politicians is in the business of discussing whether p is true or false (e.g., the proposition that homeopathy is effective), the practical consequence of which is that if they collectively hold p to be true, they will thereby approve a law sanctioning the use of homeopathic methods in the public health system. All politicians initially lean toward p. Moreover, all privately consider that the only good evidence bearing on p is evidence that supports p. There is much evidence against p, though, but they do not consider it to be probative because they fall prey to confirmation bias. Given how socially significant it is that the politicians settle on whether p is true or false on the basis of good epistemic reasons, a judge legally enforces that they use an anti-bias software that tediously obliges each politician to review all the scientific evidence for and against p. The same kind of debiasing process is replicated during group discussion. As it turns out, there is much more quality evidence against p than for p. The biased politicians realize this and, as a result, the group depolarizes toward not-p.

As BIASED POLITICIANS shows, the politicians' operative biases (namely, confirmation bias) are not enough to make the group polarize and, a fortiori, polarize in an epistemically improper manner. After all, the group depolarizes *despite* the manifestation of individual bias. This and the foregoing considerations are not meant to imply that individual heuristics and biases play no role in the epistemic appropriateness or inappropriateness of group polarization, but certainly militate in favor of modeling the epistemic properties of group polarization as irreducible properties of a group. To the extent that this is so, ceteris paribus, a collective model will have an advantage.

Notes

1. For this reason, defenders of this view would reject the plausibility of the competition thesis, CT, as applied to collective cognitive behavior. See §4.2.
2. In some cases, the available explanations within a heuristic/bias model might be problematic for various reasons, but they represent what we take to be the kind of explanation a proponent of this model will have to offer.
3. For discussion of this kind of signaling and its wider influence on democratic systems in which polarization on social media is prevalent, see Schabes (2020).
4. See Palermos (2016) for an extensive recent discussion.
5. See also Palermos (2016, 2017).
6. Cited also in Palermos (2016: 3).
7. An analogous argument can be given for epistemically adequate group polarization.

8   The Collective Virtue/
Vice Model

We turn now to the final (and our preferred) of the four candidate models of group polarization: the view that understands group polarization as a collective epistemic virtue in good cases of group polarization and as a collective epistemic vice in the bad cases. To this end, it will be helpful to first take a brief detour to elucidate in what sense, exactly, groups can be the bearers of epistemic virtues and vices.

8.1 Reductionism and Non-reductionism About Collective Epistemic Virtues and Vices

Epistemic virtues and vices are ascribed to individuals—but also often to groups. For example, investigation committees are said to be open or narrow-minded, intellectually honest or dishonest, partial or impartial, and so on (these are the collective counterparts of individual character-based virtues and vices). Similarly, research groups are said to manifest a disposition to produce accurate research outputs but also to produce flawed results (these are the collective counterparts of reliabilistically modeled individual epistemic virtues and vices).

As with other collective properties, collective epistemic virtues can be understood along summativist, reductionist lines (i.e., as mere aggregations of the epistemic virtues of individual members)—in this sense, attribution of epistemic virtues to groups is merely figurative—or else in non-reductionist terms (i.e., as non-reducible to individual features).

More precisely stated, (weak) reductionism about collective epistemic virtues and vices is the view that a group has an epistemic virtue or vice (e.g., collective open-mindedness/narrow-mindedness) just in case all or most of its members have epistemic virtues or vices of the same type (e.g., individual open-mindedness/narrow-mindedness). In other words, collective epistemic virtues and vices are nothing over and above a summation of epistemic virtues and vices. However, not all collective epistemic virtues and vices can be understood along reductionist lines. Consider the following case by Lahroodi (2007). Imagine a church committee whose members are progressive priests and nuns who are individually open-minded about gay rights (i.e., outside the group), but because of social pressures, they collectively tow the church line on gay rights so that the committee ends up (very) narrow-minded in its stances. It is not the case that if all or most members of this committee have a trait or disposition, then the group has it—because all members of the committee are open-minded, but the committee is not. Conversely, it's not the case that if this group exhibits a trait or disposition, then all or most of its members also display it—the committee is narrow-minded, but its members are not. Therefore, the collective epistemic vice of being narrow-minded would not be such that we could plausibly explain it in reductionist terms.

By contrast, non-reductionism about collective epistemic virtues and vices rejects the idea that these are summations of individual epistemic virtues and vices, in that it allows for cases like the narrow-minded church committee, in which the group has a trait (in this case an epistemic vice) that none of its members have.[1]

However, none of this tells us much about the *nature* of non-summative epistemic virtues and vices. One way to make this view more informative will be to draw from the resources of Margaret Gilbert's popular "plural subject" account (Gilbert 1989, 2006, 2000, 2017), a non-reductionist approach to group features and social phenomena in general.

According to Gilbert (2006: 144–145), several individuals constitute a plural subject just in case they jointly commit to doing something as a body—Gilbert construes "doing something" broadly to comprise actions, attitudes, or states such as beliefs, acceptances of rules of action, and the like. A *joint commitment* (Gilbert's key notion) is a commitment of two or more people in conditions of common knowledge, and as a collective commitment it is not reducible to the personal commitments of the individuals who are part of it. This irreducibility is the reason Gilbert includes the qualifier "as a body" (or "as one" or "as a whole") in her definition of plural subject. In Gilbert's own words:

> The complex idea of a joint commitment to espouse a goal as a body is to be roughly interpreted as follows. The relevant joint commitment is an instruction to the parties to see to it that they act in such a way as to emulate as best they can a single body with the goal in question.
>
> (Gilbert 2013: 33)[2]

Miranda Fricker (2010) tweaks Gilbert's plural subject view to account for collective virtues and vices, both on a character and a reliabilist framework. According to Fricker, a group G has a *collective character virtue* when G's members jointly commit to a good motive as a body (more specifically, when they jointly commit to achieving the good end of the motive *because it is good*). For example, on this kind of proposal, what makes a jury open-minded or impartial is that its members jointly commit to being open-minded or impartial as a body. Of course, this does not mean (in keeping with the non-reductionist spirit of Gilbert's plural subject account) that individual jurors need to *personally* possess such motives outside the jury. It might be the case that jurors fail to be impartial when not acting in their capacity *as* jurors, e.g., by giving weight to evidence coming from hearsay, gossip, or rumor in their personal lives. However, provided their commitments as jurors feature in a wider collective joint commitment to impartiality when they are acting *as* jurors, they must (in the sense that are normatively obliged to) rule out evidence of that sort; otherwise, they invite formal censure—or even worse—may be ousted from the relevant joint commitment and hence from the jury itself.

This should all come as no surprise. After all, as Fricker points out, we, *qua* social subjects, have various kinds of *practical identities* (i.e., obligations to act in certain ways because of being part of joint commitments). What's more, the many joint commitments we are involved in (often, unavoidably simultaneously) might end up conflicting. In Fricker's own words, "one may confront a situation, decision, or choice as a professional, *as* a parent, *as* a friend, *as* a gay man, *as* a Christian, *as* an interested or disinterested party, and so on" (Fricker 2010: 241). Sometimes, such practical identities clash with each other.

Fricker's view of *collective faculties* or *skills* (i.e., the reliabilist counterpart of collective character virtues) has it that they arise from joint commitments to achieve good ends *reliably*. Such joint commitments are not composed of, as it were, a pool of individual wills to achieve good ends out of certain motives—as in the case of collective character virtues—but are rather grounded in a pool of individual faculties in conditions of common knowledge.

As an illustration of this, Fricker uses the example of a night watch team. Suppose that each of the four sentinels of the team is individually competent at monitoring incoming foes and that the way they collectively manage this feat is by shifting their gaze randomly. In such a case, the night watch team cannot be considered reliable as a body, because it could easily be the case that it leaves areas uncovered. So it is the *distribution of individual skills* that gives rise to the collective faculty of vigilance. In particular, a more reliable division of labor would lead each sentinel to surveil only one direction (e.g., North, South, East, and West).[3] Furthermore, if it is the distribution of skills that gives rise to the collective skill, it is in principle possible for a group to be competent even if its members are not, on the proviso that the group's structure or organization makes the pooling of individual dispositions sufficiently reliable. To see this, consider the *catenaccio* defensive strategy in soccer, an ultra-defensive tactical system that organizes team players in a solid backline defense with the only aim of thwarting the goal chances of the opposing team while increasing the chances of counterattacking using long passes from the defense. The system has proven effective in the past, but more importantly, does not require very skilled players.[4] It is the distribution of players on the field that does the trick.[5]

As a final note, one should keep in mind that Fricker makes two important caveats to Gilbert's requirement that the relevant joint commitments must originate in conditions of common knowledge—caveats the addition of which lead Fricker to depart from Gilbert's plural subject account in a significant way. In particular, Gilbert's common knowledge requirement entails that the relevant joint commitment be unanimous among group members and that they are self-aware in their commitment. Fricker first takes issue with the last bit: it would be too strained to require for collective virtue that group members are self-aware of their motives and goals. After all, individuals need not be aware of (in the sense that they do not need to conceptualize) the motives or goals that define their virtues or their reliability for that matter (e.g., virtues such as modesty or vigilance fit this profile). By the looks of it, then, the self-awareness requirement is one that Fricker opts to drop. The second of Fricker's caveats is that we should relax Gilbert's *unanimity requirement* on joint commitment, as this is at odds with the non-summativist idea that groups can have virtues without most or all of their members possessing them. To account for such possible cases, Fricker introduces the idea of "*passengers*", namely group members who either go along with the motives and goals of a subgroup or with externally imposed procedures that establish a joint commitment that promotes such motives or goods. Either way, passengers' joint commitment to go along suffices for the group to exhibit a virtue, according to Fricker.

What about *collective vices*? Here Fricker's account mirrors her account of collective virtues. In the case of collective faculties or skills, corresponding collective vices are explained in terms of joint commitments that fail to exhibit a sufficient degree of reliability in achieving the relevant collective goals. For example, a poorly organized night watch team would fit this profile, in that the group itself is collectively unreliable when it comes to surveillance.

In the case of collective traits, Fricker thinks that a group has a collective character vice when its members jointly commit to achieving the end of a bad motive *because it is bad*. In other words, Fricker locates the source of a group's epistemic vice in a *positive* orientation toward bad epistemic goals. But there are reasons to doubt this more generally. In particular, in the same way as some individual epistemic vices (e.g., intellectual laziness, intellectual cowardice) cannot be accounted for in terms of a positive orientation toward epistemically bad ends but in terms of a lack of appropriate desire or motivation for epistemic goods (e.g., Zagzebski 1996; Montmarquet 1993; Baehr 2011), some collective epistemic vices such as group intellectual laziness or collective intellectual cowardice can only be explained likewise. And the same plausibly goes for what Tanesini (2018) calls *collective amnesia*, where collective memories are shaped by ignorance-promoting mechanisms that may—but need not—involve any deliberate intention to mislead.[6]

8.2 The View in Outline

8.2.1 The Case Against the Character-based Framework

With Fricker's account of collective virtues and vices now in view, let's consider how epistemically virtuous and vicious group polarization might be accounted for. And here there are two general possibilities that correspond with the reliabilist and character-based frameworks of collective virtues and vices.

From a *reliabilist* perspective, a group G virtuously polarizes if and only if G's members are jointly committed to achieving epistemically good ends reliably. By contrast, G viciously polarizes if G's members are *not* jointly committed to achieving epistemically good ends reliably—where this can be because no joint commitment exists among G's members or because they are jointly committed to achieving epistemically good ends *unreliably*, which is admittedly a rarer (yet possible) case.

From a *character-based* perspective, a group G virtuously polarizes if and only if G's members are jointly committed to achieving epistemically good ends because of being positively motivated by that goodness. By contrast, a group G viciously polarizes if (i) either G's members are jointly committed to achieving epistemically bad ends because of being negatively motivated by that badness or (ii) they are *not* jointly committed to achieving epistemically good ends because of being positively motivated by that goodness.

A relevant question at this juncture, of course, is: what epistemic end or goal, exactly, is such that are members of polarized groups are jointly committed to (or fail to be jointly committed to) bring it about? One obvious candidate is *truth*. Now, if truth is the relevant epistemic end, which we plausibly think it is (see, e.g., Goldman 1999), we can rule out the character-based framework out of hand as a plausible way to conceptualize group polarization in terms of collective epistemic virtues and vices.

First, it is both possible that a polarized group is epistemically vicious and that their members are jointly committed to achieving true group views by having the right kind of *positive motivation* toward the goodness of that goal. For example, it is plausible, indeed, that the empirical studies that have found polarization effects in groups whose task is to discuss *factual* questions are such that the subjects are positively motivated toward settling on correct views. However, the relevant polarization in such groups might be due to, among other things, normative factors, such as social comparison or self-categorization processes. As argued in Chapter 3, such factors, being non-epistemic, make group polarization epistemically inappropriate and thereby not epistemically virtuous. Besides, the fact that Federal judges polarize in their decisions when engaged in group discussion (see Chapter 2) is more compatible with the hypothesis that they are positively motivated toward reaching verdicts based on facts—and thus toward finding the truth—rather than with the opposite hypothesis. Still, they might polarize due, in part, to non-epistemic factors and hence in a non-epistemically virtuous way.

A defender of the character-based framework might attempt to press back here as follows: group polarization (in the bad cases) is on a par with collective epistemic vices such as collective intellectual cowardice or collective amnesia, in the sense that the correct way to model them (on a character framework) is not in terms of group members being jointly committed toward a bad epistemic end by being *negatively motivated* toward it, but in terms of group members lacking a joint commitment toward epistemically good ends thereby *lacking* the right kind of *positive motivation*.

However, it's hard to see how this could be the right way to model group polarization in the bad cases. After all, if lack of joint commitment toward an epistemically good end, particularly, truth, is sufficient for group polarization's being epistemically vicious, then some paradigmatic cases of virtuous group polarization will plausibly not count as such, such as our paradigm case of virtuous group polarization: GOOD SCIENTISTS (see §3.3)

As we've described the case, the good scientists make sure to find and share only good evidence and are only driven by truth-related considerations during deliberation. However, this is compatible with two kinds of motivations: (i) a purely *epistemic* motivation toward the truth and (ii) a *pragmatic* motivation toward non-epistemic goals in such a way that achieving true group views is merely taken to be instrumental to them. For example, the fact that the good scientists virtuously polarize—because all their actions are epistemically impeccable—is compatible with the fact that they are primarily motivated (individually or collectively) toward gaining recognition and improving their reputation, where reaching *true* collective views is the best way toward achieving those non-epistemic goals. On a character-based framework, such pragmatic motivation would count as epistemically vicious *even if* the good scientists clearly outperform groups whose members individually or collectively have a sincere desire for settling on true views but nevertheless fall prey to the influence of normative factors such as social comparison or self-categorization processes. This result strikes us as plainly wrong. Individual or collective motivation should play no role in adjudicating between virtuous and vicious polarization.

This paves the way for a reliabilist understanding of virtuous and vicious group polarization. Indeed, from a reliabilist perspective, group polarization can be conceptualized as a collective epistemic vice regardless of individual or collective motivations if it falls short of reliability *qua* process of collective belief formation and as an epistemic virtue otherwise. What does it mean, exactly, that group polarization is "reliable" or "unreliable"? We take up this question in the next section.

8.2.2 The (Irrelevant) Conditional Reliability of Group Polarization

One simple view about group polarization is that it is a *belief-dependent process* in that it takes the beliefs of group members before deliberation as the input to its operation—namely, the average pre-deliberation belief—and delivers a more extreme average belief as output after deliberation. As Goldman (2014) points out, *unconditional reliability* (high ratio of true beliefs to total beliefs) is an inappropriate standard for a belief-dependent process; instead, we should assess them according to their *conditional reliability*. Here's Goldman (2014):

> A given inference type might generate a great many false conclusion beliefs because it is often applied to false premise beliefs. This would not demonstrate any defect in the inference type. We can define a notion of conditional reliability, however, that supplies a more appropriate criterion. A process is conditionally reliable only if it has a high ratio of true belief outputs to total belief outputs for those cases in which the inputs to the process are (all) true.
>
> (2014: 15)

Like inference, group polarization—understood as a kind of collective belief-dependent process—can be assessed for conditional reliability rather than unconditional unreliability so that if a group has a high ratio of true pre-deliberation beliefs and polarizes, it will have a high ratio of true post-deliberation beliefs, too, and *vice versa*: if it has a high ratio of false pre-deliberation beliefs and polarizes, it will have a high ratio of false post-deliberation beliefs. Collective garbage in, collective garbage out.

Group polarization is thus conditionally reliable in Goldman's sense. More specifically, a belief-forming process involving group polarization is conditionally reliable if and only if it has a high (enough) ratio of true belief outputs to total belief outputs for those cases in which the inputs to the process are (all) true.[7] There should be nothing surprising here. The conditional reliability of group polarization derives from the more general fact that polarizing, in general, involves moving to the near or already preferred pole: if a group leans toward a true or a false view, group polarization will only exacerbate such leaning.

That said, conditional reliability understood in the aforementioned way is not relevant for the purposes of establishing whether group polarization is a collective epistemic virtue (or vice, for that matter). The reason is that there are conditionally reliable belief-forming processes that we would hardly consider epistemic virtues. By way of illustration, just compare the following two subjects. Subject 1 is endowed with excellent inferential capacities (e.g., at logic) and can thereby be (rightly) described as epistemically virtuous when drawing inferences by modus tollens. By contrast, subject 2 is *not* able to draw inferences of the form p entails q and not-q, therefore not-p. Suppose that subject 2 implements the following method of belief formation: for any propositions p, q, whenever she forms the true beliefs that not-q and that p entails q, someone beats her over the head, making her believe not-p. This (luckily) always happens, and the resulting not-p beliefs are invariably true. Like the inferential capacities of subject 1, this method is conditionally reliable—even more than the former—but the belief-forming method here is clearly not epistemically virtuous.[8] The point, more explicitly, is that mere conditional reliability does not serve to adjudicate between epistemically virtuous and vicious belief-forming processes, whether individual or collective.

The connection between conditional reliability and virtue is tenuous, indeed. Another analogy to the individual level will bring this point into sharp relief. Take the vice of individual-level gullibility—viz., a disposition to uncritically accept testimony as true even if there are indicators present to the contrary. Gullibility is paradigmatically an epistemic vice. And yet, gullibility is conditionally reliable. If one so happens to be in a maximally benevolent epistemic environment, a reliable route to forming true beliefs is to trust blindly, taking as input the true beliefs of others, without scrutiny. This is the case, to be clear, even in circumstances in which one does not realize one's environment is maximally epistemically friendly. The fact that gullibility is conditionally reliable in the respect just noted is not a good reason to suppose that we have been wrong to think of gullibility as a vice. A more general point here is that a trait's being such that it maximizes accuracy in highly idealized situations (e.g., when inputs are ideal) does not suffice to tell us whether that trait is a virtue or a vice. Instead, what matters is reliability in normal conditions; normally, the kinds of idealized circumstances under which gullibility is truth-conducive are rare, which is why this is not a good trait to have from the point of view where getting to the truth is what matters. What goes for gullibility at the individual level goes, mutatis mutandis, for group polarization at the collective level.

8.2.3 The Goals and Competences of Epistemically Virtuous and Vicious Polarized Groups

According to the reliabilist, non-reductionist framework of collective epistemic virtues and vices, a group G virtuously polarizes if and only if G's members are jointly committed to achieving epistemically good ends reliably. By contrast, G viciously polarizes if G's members are *not* jointly committed to achieving epistemically good ends reliably—where, as we have pointed out, this can be because no joint commitment exists among *G*'s members or because they are jointly committed to achieving epistemically good ends *unreliably*, which is admittedly a rarer (yet possible) case.

However, epistemically virtuous and vicious group polarization cannot be merely characterized as group members being (or failing to be) jointly committed to reaching *true* collective views reliably. As just argued, this reliability is to be understood as conditional reliability, because group polarization is a belief-dependent process and, in particular, a process that exacerbates the group's initial leaning. In this way, having an average pre-deliberation true belief suffices for reaching that goal reliably. However, this is compatible both with epistemically virtuous *and* vicious group polarization. Therefore, mere conditional reliability is insufficient to settle whether group polarization, understood as a belief-dependent process, is a collective epistemic virtue or a vice.

Interestingly, if we focus on our paradigm case of epistemically virtuous group polarization, GOOD SCIENTISTS, there are other good epistemic ends or goals that the good scientists *competently* pursue and *reliably* achieve. In particular:

1. **The evidential acquisition goal:** good evidence is successfully collected.
2. **The evidential filtering goal:** bad evidence is successfully filtered out so that it does not enter group discussion.
3. **The evidential assessment goal:** the confirmational import of the private and shared evidence is correctly assessed.
4. **The evidential disclosure goal:** privately possessed good evidence is fully disclosed during group deliberation.
5. **The non-epistemic influences filtering goal:** non-epistemic factors are successfully prevented from influencing group deliberation.
6. **The evidential scrutiny goal:** good counterevidence against the beliefs of individual members is searched and discussed and its confirmational import correctly assessed, and the most plausible ways to prove the beliefs of group members wrong are examined.

By taking into account these goals, we can put forward a reliabilist account of epistemically virtuous group polarization, where the reliability in question is not understood as mere conditional reliability—and specifically, in terms of conditional truth-conduciveness—but as reliability at meeting the relevant epistemic goals, i.e., in terms of unconditional goal-conduciveness. In particular:

> **Goal-reliability:** for any individual or collective method *M* for achieving epistemic goal *E*, *M* is goal-reliable if and only if its ratio of achievement of *E* to total attempts to achieve *E* (when operating in the relevant domain) is very high.[9]

The general idea, then, is that groups that are goal-reliable when polarizing—vis-à-vis the relevant epistemic goals—are thereby epistemically virtuous. Note that the relevant epistemic goals, although they are different from the standard goal of forming true rather than false individual or collective beliefs, can be instrumental to the latter, e.g., when deliberation only revolves around good evidence because the evidential filtering goal is met. Thus, the next task will be to identify the kinds of goals of the previous list that are *required* for virtuous group polarization. In GOOD SCIENTISTS, our paradigmatic case of virtuous group polarization, all the relevant goals are reliably fulfilled, but this does not imply that reliably meeting these goals is necessary for virtuous group polarization. The good scientists might well be acting in an epistemically supererogatory way—so to speak—and might end up doing more than they are epistemically required, at least when epistemically virtuous group performance is the normative standard. No doubt, this makes GOOD SCIENTISTS an exceptionally fitting instance of group polarization—one that is uniquely conducive to collective knowledge—but polarized groups can be epistemically virtuous by doing less. For example, epistemically virtuous belief-formation (whether individual or collective) is compatible with forming a false (individual or collective) belief; by contrast, knowledge (whether individual or collective) is not.

In this way, the next task is to specify which of the preceding goals befit epistemically virtuous group polarization—rather than, e.g., knowledge-able polarized group belief. Before that, two caveats are in order. The first is that, whatever those goals are, a group is not immediately epistemically vicious if, on a given occasion, it fails to satisfy the relevant epistemic goals. What matters for epistemic virtue attribution is *competence* at fulfilling the goal (viz., high ratio of success), not the actual achievement of the goal. A competence or skill to ϕ remains a competence or skill—and, therefore, a reliabilist virtue—even if on occasions one fails to ϕ. Competences are competences because they are reliable, not infallible.[10] If the epistemic standard were other than epistemic virtue, e.g., if we were assessing whether collective beliefs qualify as collective knowledge, the success dimension, as pointed out before, would be relevant (knowledge, whether individual or collective, is factive).

The second caveat is that maintaining that the reliable attainment of (some of) these goals is a hallmark of epistemically virtuous group polarization is compatible with also countenancing that truth is the most fundamental epistemic goal, i.e., with the thesis often referred to in epistemic axiology as *veritism*.[11] Independently of whether or not a group polarizes, group deliberation is more likely to produce true collective views by meeting any of these goals than by not fulfilling them. In other words, goals 1–6, when satisfied, increase the truth-conduciveness of group deliberation.

Without further ado, let now look squarely at the first epistemic goal: the *evidential acquisition goal*. Recall that one of the conclusions from

Chapter 3 was that, when it comes to group polarization, it is not as important how the evidence is *acquired* as it is how it is *distributed*. This is evidenced by the fact that groups akin to the research group of NOT-SO-GOOD SCIENTISTS manage to polarize in epistemically adequate ways *despite collecting bad evidence* (see §3.6). The reason is that the not-so-good scientists (and similar groups) are as competent as the good scientists at filtering out the bad evidence and hence at meeting the *evidential filtering goal*. Thus, by not letting any bad evidence enter group discussion (even if privately held), group deliberation solely revolves around good evidence—albeit in the case of the good scientists on *more* good evidence. Given this, a plausible thesis is the following:

> **Evidential filtering competence**: a group *G* virtuously polarizes only if *G*'s members are jointly committed to achieving the evidential filtering goal reliably.

Concerning the *evidential assessment goal*, we saw in Chapter 3 that correctly judging the confirmational import of the evidence is crucial for epistemically appropriate polarization: the various ways of misjudging the confirmational import of the evidence that we distinguished have a negative impact on the group members' pre-deliberation and post-deliberation beliefs as well as on whether or not group members share their private evidence with other group members. Accordingly, another plausible condition on epistemically virtuous group polarization is the following:

> **Evidential assessment competence**: a group *G* virtuously polarizes only if *G*'s members are jointly committed to achieving the evidential assessment goal reliably.

Regarding the *evidential disclosure goal*, we saw in Chapter 3 that it is not as important that all the good evidence is put on the table as it is that privately possessed bad evidence (if any) does not enter group discussion. In particular, in situations where a group's pool of evidence is comprised of both good and bad evidence, not sharing good evidence might cause trouble if bad evidence enters group discussion and the good evidence is such that, were to be disclosed, it would defeat the bad evidence. The problem, however, is not that good evidence is not shared but rather that *bad evidence enters group discussion* in the first place. Accordingly, it is more reasonable that groups that virtuously polarize must possess a competence to filter out the bad evidence (i.e., an evidential filtering competence) rather than a competence to fully disclose their good evidence.

A different issue arises when *non-epistemic factors influence group deliberation*, such as social comparison or self-categorization processes. In such cases, as argued in Chapter 3, group polarization becomes epistemically problematic. Plausibly, groups that virtuously polarize have mechanisms to cancel out such non-epistemic influences:

> **Non-epistemic influences filtering competence**: a group G virtuously polarizes only if G's members are jointly committed to achieving the non-epistemic influences filtering goal reliably.

Finally, we also saw in Chapter 3 that, on some occasions, there is *evidence groups ought to discuss* such that a failure to do so bears negatively on the epistemic adequacy of group polarization. We saw, in particular, that if a group polarizes toward p drawing only (or mainly) on good evidence for p but there is good evidence against p that group members ought to have discussed but have not—or if they discuss it but fail to see its confirmational import—the polarization of such a group is not epistemically proper. Accordingly, groups that virtuously polarize are competent at scrutinizing possible counterevidence:

> **Evidential scrutinizing competence**: a group G virtuously polarizes only if G's members are jointly committed to achieving the evidential scrutiny goal reliably.

This completes our account of virtuous group polarization:

> **Virtuous group polarization**: a group G virtuously polarizes if and only if G's members are jointly committed to achieving the evidential filtering, the evidential assessment, the non-epistemic influences filtering, and the evidential scrutiny goals reliably.

To put it another way, polarized groups are epistemically virtuous if and only if they are endowed with evidential filtering, evidential assessing, non-epistemic influences filtering, and evidential scrutinizing competences. Correspondingly, when a group that polarizes is not reliable with respect to the epistemic goals that are constitutive of these competences, it is epistemically vicious. More specifically:

> **Vicious group polarization**: a group G viciously polarizes if G's members are *not* jointly committed to achieving either the evidential filtering, the evidential assessment, the non-epistemic influences filtering, or the evidential scrutiny goals reliably—or if they adopt joint commitments that subvert the reliable achievement of such goals.

In other words, polarized groups are epistemically vicious if they lack evidential filtering, evidential assessing, non-epistemic influences filtering *or* evidential scrutinizing competences, or when, even if they have them,

other joint commitments adopted by group members make such competences futile—see the following DECEIVED GOOD SCIENTISTS case
for an example.

The kind of view we've advanced in this section is *reliabilist* in that it
does not require that group members or that the group itself exhibit any
sort of motivation toward good epistemic ends but only that the group
is goal-reliable with respect to the epistemic goals that are constitutive
of the kind of competences, we think, epistemically virtuous polarized
groups manifest. Of course, this represents a substantial departure from
extant reliabilist views of epistemic virtues (namely, the fact that reliability, understood as per truth-conduciveness, is not all that matters). However, this further complexity that our view introduces—namely, the fact
that it's built upon a different notion of reliability, viz., goal-reliability—is
reflective of the (enormous) complexity of the kind of collective phenomenon we are theorizing about (group polarization). This, however, does
not transform our view into a kind of "impure" reliabilist view but into
a richer kind of reliabilism. Reliability, after all, is just a way to measure
success and failure with respect to some goal in a given domain, and,
when it comes to epistemic matters, there are various kinds of epistemic
goals other than the goal of acquiring true rather than false beliefs. Of
course, this is not to say that the latter should not be considered the most
fundamental goal in epistemology (as the veritist has it) or for that matter to deny that the former are valuable only as long as they are instrumental to maximizing truth or minimizing falsehood. Rather, the idea is
that many goals other than truth can (and should) be taken into account
when disentangling the complexity of epistemically interesting phenomena (especially collective phenomena) in pure and simple (albeit perhaps
not traditional) reliabilist terms.[12]

8.2.4 The Multiple Possibilities of Non-reductionism

Unlike the reductive virtue/vice model, our account of virtuous and
vicious group polarization is *non-reductionist*. This has immediate consequences. Like the former, non-reductionism about collective epistemic
virtues is compatible with countenancing that *all or most individual
group members* are epistemically virtuous. In this way, a group *G* may
have a competence *C* when all group members are jointly committed to
achieving the kind of goal that is constitutive of *C* reliably, where this
can be grounded on the fact that all of them are individually competent
at achieving that goal. For example, if a sufficient number of individual
members are individually competent at (and hence jointly committed to)
assessing the confirmational import of the evidence, the group thereby
possesses a corresponding evidential assessment competence. If the same
is the case for the rest of epistemic goals that are constitutive of virtuous
group polarization, the fact that all group members are competent at the

individual level may explain (on a non-reductionist model) collectively virtuous and hence epistemically appropriate group polarization. Likewise, vicious group polarization can be fruitfully explained, on a non-reductionist model, in terms of the fact that less than all or most group members fail to be jointly committed to achieving one such epistemic goal.

However, an interesting feature of non-reductionism about collective epistemic virtues—and what distinguishes it from the reductive virtue/vice model—is that it is also compatible with groups being (i) epistemically virtuous when *no* individual group member possesses corresponding individual competences and (ii) epistemically vicious when *all* group members are competent.

Concerning (i), in particular, group members can be jointly committed to a reliable method for reaching the kind of goal that is constitutive of the relevant competence without being themselves individually competent in that way. By way of illustration, consider the evidential filtering goal in the case of group polarization. One way in which a group can be competent at meeting this goal is that group members are jointly committed to using software that, they know, prevents bad evidence from entering group discussion. For example, group interaction can be computer-mediated in such a way that group discussion is exclusively fed with information coming from trustworthy sources, such as peer-reviewed journals or with evidence produced by reliable methods, such as randomized clinical trials.

Concerning (ii), consider a version of GOOD SCIENTISTS in which, as in the original case, all group members are individually competent at achieving the evidential filtering, the evidential assessment, the non-epistemic influences filtering, and the evidential scrutiny goals. In the envisaged version (call it DECEIVED GOOD SCIENTISTS), the competent scientists, having found no good counterevidence against the group's dominant view, want to double-check whether there is any good counterevidence they might have missed. To that aim, they jointly commit to using a seemingly reliable software that feeds group discussion with seemingly good counterevidence. In reality, however, such software has been specifically engineered to deceive them (e.g., by Big Pharma) to flood group discussion with fabricated evidence and make the group adopt views that favor financial rather than epistemic interests. Despite the scientists' reliable capacities for assessing the evidence's confirmational import, the counterevidence provided by the software is tailored in such a convincing way that, each time the group engages in deliberation, the scientists end up giving higher credence to the allegedly good counterevidence than to the good evidence collected. As a result, the group always ends up polarizing—but in the opposite direction, i.e., toward falsehoods. The bottom line, then, is that, once the group adopts the joint (and hence collective) commitment to using the software in question, the epistemic goodness that the scientists' individual competences bring about is effectively "canceled out" by the epistemic badness that the fabricated evidence of the malicious software gives rise to. Unsurprisingly, the scientists polarize in an epistemically vicious and hence epistemically problematic way.

The non-reductionist component of our account thus allows for multiple possibilities, namely (i) epistemically virtuous group polarization due to the individual competences of group members but also to epistemically positive joint commitments in the absence of individual competences and (ii) epistemically vicious group polarization due to the lack of individual competences among group members but also to epistemically negative joint commitments despite the presence of individual competences.

In fact, our model *might* even be compatible with epistemically virtuous cases of *outsourced competences*. For example, the members of a group (e.g., politicians) might need to settle on a collective view that falls out of their area of expertise. To assess the confirmational import of their evidence (and possible counterevidence) as well as to judge whether such evidence is good or bad, they might hire external experts to write a report on what exactly the group's evidence (and possible counterevidence) shows. Group deliberation, drawing on the results of such an externally sourced report, might lead to group polarization. On a plausible interpretation of this case, this ensuing polarization is *epistemically virtuous*, insofar as group members are jointly committed to a reliable *outsourced* method for meeting the evidential filtering, assessment, and scrutiny goals—suppose that the group counts with reliable mechanisms for canceling out normative influences. Nonetheless, we might want to impose more restrictive conditions to cases of outsourced competences than to competences that groups possess, such as the requirement that group members must have knowledge or a justified belief that the outsourced method is reliable.[13] In the previous example, this is the case.

Admittedly, the conditions we are putting forward for epistemically virtuous group polarization are not by any means easy to satisfy. If *social comparison* and *self-categorization theories* are right that normative influences normally contribute to group polarization, real-life groups often polarize in an epistemically vicious way. For it suffices that non-epistemic factors are present during group deliberation to render the resulting polarization of a group epistemically vicious. After all, the presence of such factors is indicative of a lack of non-epistemic influences filtering competence.

However, even if social comparison and self-categorization theories are wrong and only *persuasive arguments theory* is right in that group polarization is solely caused by informational influences (viz., epistemic factors), we still have shown three relevant ways in which polarized groups can go haywire *epistemically*. To put it another way, even if polarized groups are competent at preventing non-epistemic factors from influencing group deliberation, they can still polarize in epistemically vicious ways, namely by being *in*competent (i) at filtering out their bad private evidence, (ii) at correctly judging the confirmational import of the evidence, or (iii) at searching, discussing, and correctly assessing good counterevidence against the beliefs of individual members (when there is an epistemic obligation to do it) as well as examining the most plausible ways to disprove such beliefs. Given how demanding it can be for a group to possess *all* these epistemic competences and given how often non-epistemic factors pollute group deliberation, epistemically virtuous group polarization is going to be found in real life only in the best epistemic circles, such as those of science, academic research, or other kinds of skilled expert deliberations. This is not to say that groups of scientists, researchers and, in general, experts do not fall prey to epistemically vicious group polarization (or that no other groups could fail to do so). They often do. The claim is rather just that if epistemically virtuous group polarization is to be found in real life, it will likely be in such groups. And indeed, this is exactly what we should expect.

8.2.5 False Pre-deliberation Beliefs and Collective Epistemic Virtues

One might still wonder what the relationship between epistemically virtuous group polarization and *falsehood* is. In particular, what happens when the pre-deliberation beliefs of groups are false? Can they be epistemically virtuous in the way we have proposed?

Our view about epistemically virtuous and vicious group polarization is a view about collective competences (and lack thereof). As we've noted, competences are reliable but not infallible. This fallibility means that, on at least some occasions, groups with the required competences can possibly polarize and deliver false post-deliberation outputs, which means in turn that the corresponding average pre-deliberation beliefs will be false. This will seldom happen, however.

Epistemically virtuous groups that start with dominant false beliefs have at least two mechanisms for *not* polarizing. For instance, suppose that the dominant pre-deliberation belief of an epistemically virtuous group is false because their members have acquired and unluckily followed misleading evidence, e.g., evidence from a fraudulent clinical trial published in an obscure journal. One thing group members can do to avoid polarizing toward that falsehood is use the group's evidential filtering competences. Such competences, if successfully deployed, prevent the initial misleading evidence from entering group discussion. As we have argued, this does not require that group members must be *individually* competent at recognizing the bad evidence and hence at filtering it out. In fact, the fact that they are individually *in*competent at detecting the bad evidence may be the cause of the group's average pre-deliberation false belief. Still, group members can be jointly committed to a method that does the filtering work reliably, such as software that rules out specific journals as trustworthy or expert reports that reliably evaluate the quality of the group members' private evidence.

Besides, even if the initial bad evidence manages to sneak into group discussion, the envisaged epistemically virtuous group can put its evidential scrutinizing competences to work. Such competences (again, they need not be individual competences) can bring good evidence against the group members' beliefs into discussion. For example, they can result in group members discussing a meta-analysis showing that the results of the clinical trial that misleadingly led them to form, on average, a false pre-deliberation belief are in plain conflict with the best available evidence.

The most probable outcome in cases such as the one just considered is that group members will ultimately suspend judgment on the issue in question and that the group will not thereby polarize in the wrong direction. Sometimes, of course, the competences of a virtuous group may fail to meet the goals they are aimed at, so that the group may end up with a more extreme false post-deliberation belief, but this is due (once again) to the fact that competences, in general, are reliable, not infallible. Compare: even the most reliable individual perceiver might form a false perceptually based belief in highly unusual circumstances or due to extremely bad environmental luck.

8.3 Solving the Problems: The Scoreboard

In what follows, we will briefly explain how the collective virtue/vice model is poised to steer clear of the other three views' problems. Let us start with the objections raised against the reductive virtue/vice model (the view that group polarization is to be explained as a summation of individual vices). To this view, we raised three key problems: the *pessimism problem* (i.e., the problem of dispersing epistemic viciousness too widely), the *individual blamelessness problem* (i.e., the problem of accounting for individual group members blamelessly updating their credences in light of new information), and the *Mandevillian intelligence problem* (i.e., the problem of explaining cases of collective virtues that arise out of a distribution of individual vices).

More specifically, concerning the *pessimism problem*, our model does not, as the reductive virtue/vice view does, spread epistemic viciousness too widely because it locates virtue and vice at the collective level—and irreducibly so—in terms of a lack of joint commitment to reliably achieving the evidential filtering, the evidential assessment, the non-epistemic influences filtering, and the evidential scrutiny goals—or else in terms of the existence of joint commitments that subvert such goals. As argued in §8.2.4, collective epistemic viciousness might be explained by the fact that group members are individually vicious, but *this need not be the case*. The collective virtue/vice model, in virtue of being a non-reductionist proposal, allows for the possibility that epistemically negative joint commitments are the source of epistemically vicious group polarization *even when* individual group members are competent. For example, in DECEIVED GOOD SCIENTISTS, the problem is not that the scientists are individually incompetent but that they jointly commit to using malicious software that systematically leads them to polarize toward false group views.

The collective virtue/vice model, precisely because it allows for the existence of cases of epistemically vicious group polarization in which all group members are individually competent in the relevant way, can straightforwardly address the *individual blamelessness problem* as well. In particular, it can account for the intuition that competent group members are blameless for updating their beliefs in light of new supporting information. In DECEIVED GOOD SCIENTISTS, for example, the scientists are excused and are therefore blameless for giving higher credence to the allegedly good counterevidence provided by the malicious software than to the good evidence they have collected. After all, such software is specifically engineered to deceive them, just as vats are specifically engineered (at least by epistemologists) to deceive brains.

Finally, concerning the *Mandevillian intelligence problem*, our model—given that it is non-reductive—is certainly not at odds with the idea that a well-organized distribution of individual vices could give rise to a genuinely collective virtue, and accordingly to epistemically virtuous group polarization. For instance, as we have seen, dogmatic individual-level tendencies among group members, when adequately organized in the way envisaged by Zollman (2010) and Smart (2018), contribute fruitfully to group-level accuracy in a way that runs counter to epistemically bad polarization. This is certainly licensed by Fricker's account of collective skills or competences (Fricker 2010), on which the model is based. As argued in §8.1, Fricker's view is compatible with the possibility that a group is competent (i.e., epistemically virtuous) even if its individual members are not, on the proviso that the group's structure or organization makes the pooling of individual dispositions sufficiently reliable. We gave the *catenaccio* example as an illustration of this, and there is no principled reason why analogous cases of epistemically unproblematic group polarization should not be understood likewise.

Let's now turn to the collective heuristic/bias model. The collective heuristic/bias model faced an *empirical adequacy* problem: it maintains that epistemically inappropriate group polarization is due to a collective bias, but empirical psychologists *do not* consider it as such, i.e., among the kind of phenomena that psychologists describe as "collective biases" we just don't find the kind of dynamics that give rise to group polarization. We offered similar considerations concerning the collective heuristic/bias model's explanation of epistemically appropriate group polarization in terms of fast-and-frugal collective heuristics. The collective virtue/vice model fails to run afoul of empirical adequacy in two ways; first, as its central terms are not psychological terms, what matters for empirical adequacy is not "correspondence" with psychological conceptions of virtue and vice (cf., the heuristic/bias view) but rather *compatibility* with what psychology says about other things—and here there was no such incompatibility and thus no problematic empirical inadequacy.

Another problem facing the collective heuristic/bias model was that it is strained to explain epistemically inadequate group polarization in terms of a collective *bias*, insofar as biases are automatic type-1-like processes, whereas group polarization is enhanced by *type-2-like deliberation*. The collective virtue/vice model does not face this problem, because the view is compatible with the many ways in which deliberation, a paradigmatic type-2 process, can give rise to group polarization; for example, it is compatible with the fact that group members *consciously reflect* (as it often happens) on the evidence shared by others during group discussion, on the confirmational import of their own evidence, or on the validity of their own beliefs in light of the fact that fellow members are in agreement or not. After all, conscious reflection on such elements, whether reliable or not, involves type-2 processing, and the same applies to some relevant joint commitments group members might adopt—such as the conscious commitment to resort to software that screens out unreliable evidential sources.

For the very same reason the collective virtue/vice model steers clear of the *polarization entrepreneurs objection* to the reductive heuristic/bias model. The crux of the objection was that the sort of type-2 rational planning of polarization entrepreneurs is at odds with the automatic individual biases that cause group polarization. Nothing of what our preferred model says is incompatible with naturally treating the type-2 machinations of polarization entrepreneurs as one relevant factor in the explanation of why groups fail to achieve the joint commitments to the relevant epistemic goals that are constitutive of epistemically appropriate group polarization. Indeed, as we have seen, this is what seems to happen in polarized extremist groups such as terrorist organizations, where group leaders typically attenuate group dissent in order to infuse their own views and enhance polarization. For all we've said, the collective virtue/vice model can simply remain neutral on the matter of what the supervenience base of group polarization consists in. Its metaphysical commitment is to the irreducibility of group polarization—understood as a collective epistemic phenomenon (namely, a collective epistemic virtue or vice)—to that supervenience base.

The other problem we identified for the reductive heuristic/bias model was the *irreducibility problem*. The collective virtue/vice model does not succumb to this problem because it does not impose any constraint on the features individual members of a group must have in order for the group to polarize in an epistemically appropriate or inappropriate way. In this way, it does not imply that the epistemic adequacy or inadequacy of group polarization can be reduced to the epistemically adequate or inadequate individual contributions of group members. Indeed, the model's explanation of epistemically vicious group polarization in terms of the absence of joint commitments to achieving the relevant epistemic goals reliably (or else in terms of the existence of joint commitments that subvert such goals) is compatible with several structural features of the group's being the cause that such joint commitments are adopted or not.

It's time to take a look at the scoreboard. And—let there be no suspense—the collective virtue/vice model is the clear winner (see Figure 8.1); it succumbs to none of the problems canvassed and that seemed, if not intractable, at least very difficult for each of the competitor views to overcome without incurring some heavy theoretical costs elsewhere.

This comparative advantage over the other proposals, however, does not mean that the other views are plainly "wrong". Again, we do not envisage these views as positing necessary and sufficient conditions for group polarization—most likely a fool's errand—but rather as models aiming to uncover most illuminating and interesting factors in the explanation of the metaphysics and epistemology of group polarization. But of course, that a given salient factor stands out in the explanation of a phenomenon is compatible with other factors nonetheless doing some explanatory work. In this respect, while (for instance) a summation of individual epistemic virtues and vices (the reductive virtue/vice model)—or else of heuristics and biases (the reductive heuristic/bias model)—is certainly not the key factor that accounts for the metaphysics and epistemology of group polarization, it might nonetheless be the case that individual epistemic virtues and vices (or heuristics and biases) to some (non-negligible) extent account for why individuals in group settings with the characteristics of polarized groups form or fail to form the relevant joint commitments that characterize epistemically virtuous and vicious group polarization.

Indeed, as just stated, the collective virtue/vice model is neutral about what the supervenience base of group polarization is and, in particular, about what sort of model should explain *individual* cognitive behavior: a virtue/vice model or a heuristic/bias model or, perhaps, both. The advantage of this neutrality is that supporters of the collective virtue/vice model will just choose whatever model of individual cognitive behavior is empirically adequate.

	Pessimism Problem	Individual Blamelessness Problem	Mandevillian Intelligence Problem	Empirical Adequacy Problem	Type-1/ Type2 Problem	Polarization Entrepreneurs Problem	Irreducibility Problem
The Reductive Virtue/Vice Model	x	x	x				
The Collective Heuristic/Bias Model				x	x		
The Reductive Heuristic/Bias Model						x	x
The Collective Virtue/Vice Model	✓	✓	✓	✓	✓	✓	✓

Figure 8.1 Scoreboard

By contrast, the collective virtue/vice view is not neutral about genuinely collective cognitive behavior. For this reason, although it might be reconciled with the reductive virtue/vice and heuristic/bias models, it cannot be reconciled with the collective heuristic/bias model, the view that the epistemic adequacy or inadequacy of group polarization is to be explained in terms of an irreducible collective heuristic or bias. In other words, the collective virtue/vice and heuristic/bias models are in direct competition. A quick look at the scoreboard helps draw an immediate conclusion: the collective virtue/vice model wins.

Notes

1. As we anticipated §4.1, that a group feature cannot be *reduced* to a summation of individual features does not imply that it cannot supervene on individual features. For example, the supervenience base of the church committee's narrow-mindedness may comprise the respective dispositions of individual members to tow the church line. Crucially, however, collective narrow-mindedness does not reduce—and hence cannot be identified—with a summation of such dispositions.
2. Gilbert, foreseeing possible objections targeting the specific features that individuals should have in order for a joint commitment to arise, makes the following qualification:

   > The idea of a single goal-endorsing body is not itself understood in collective terms. The concept of a body that endorses a goal is neutral with respect to the nature of the goal endorser and *with respect to its composition.*
   >
   > (emphasis added; Gilbert 2013: 33)

   This leaves room for several views on what kind of individual features agents should have to be part of a joint commitment.
3. In this way, we do not need to attribute any virtuous motives to the sentinels to deem the night-watch team vigilant. What is required is that they jointly commit to achieving the end of vigilance through an available reliable method (e.g., by an effective division of labor).
4. See Orejan (2011: 103–107).
5. In fact, one way to interpret cases of this sort is as follows: individual vices outside the group (e.g., not very reliable individual capacities) no longer count as vices relative to the group insofar as the function they fulfill for the collective is conducive to the achievement of the collective's goal.
6. It is an open question whether this lack of joint commitment is to be conceptualized as an all-or-nothing affair or else as a gradual matter, in the sense that group members are either jointly committed to achieving X or not, or else their level of joint commitment is or is not sufficient (perhaps given some threshold) for counting as being committed to achieving X as a group.
7. Note that Goldman only provides a necessary condition for conditional reliability, which means that he does not exclude the fact that more conditions might be required for considering a belief-forming process conditionally reliable. Interestingly, when it comes to unconditional reliability, Goldman does provide necessary and sufficient conditions: "A process is unconditionally reliable just in case its ratio of true beliefs to total beliefs (when operating in the relevant domain) is very high" (Goldman 2014: 14).

8. For a similar kind of case, see Duncan Pritchard's case of "Temp", whose temperature-based beliefs are always true whenever he consults a broken thermometer but only due to the fortuitous intervention, unbeknownst to him, of a beneficent helper who changes the ambient temperature to correspond to whatever the broken thermometer happens to say whenever Temp consults it.
9. Note the parallel with Goldman's definition of unconditional reliability (see note 7 in this chapter).
10. See, e.g., Sosa's (2015) discussion of competent basketball shots that nonetheless miss as a kind of performative analogy to competent false belief.
11. See Goldman (1999) for a statement of this view; cf. Kelp (2014) for criticism.
12. For a similar approach to the epistemology of deliberation in general, see Broncano-Berrocal and Carter (forthcoming).
13. For an analogous kind of epistemic condition on outsourced and "extended" (i.e., Clark & Chalmers 1998) abilities in the individual case, see Prichard (2010).

9 Mitigating the Epistemic Pitfalls of Group Polarization

Should we, from an epistemic perspective, avoid group polarization altogether? Our answer is "no". To think otherwise is initially tempting when we think about paradigmatic cases of group polarization (e.g., Facebook and Twitter Trump feuds), but it's a mistake nonetheless. What we should avoid is *epistemically inappropriate* group polarization. After all, if one's group is such that deliberation is carried out in an epistemically respectable manner and, as a result, the group's view slants closer to the truth, what's wrong with that?

For example, if a research team does everything by the book from an epistemic point of view and holding internal discussion then leads the group's view to shift in the direction of what is true, why should we think that polarizing is something that the group should not be doing?

Polarization, as we saw in Chapter 3, is—intrinsically—an epistemically neutral phenomenon. It is the epistemic status of the factors that make groups polarize that turns group polarization into an epistemically problematic or unproblematic phenomenon. Accordingly, the question is not what groups should do not to polarize, but what should they do not to polarize in an epistemically bad manner.

Bearing this in mind, in this final chapter we turn to a note of constructive optimism: modeling group polarization along the lines of the collective virtue/vice model, it turns out, not only affords us a fruitful way to think about both the metaphysics and epistemology of group polarization, but it also helps us bring into view what it would take to potentially *overcome*—or at least mitigate—the epistemic pitfalls of group polarization, when things go south.

9.1 Methodological Preliminaries

Let's begin with a few preliminary points about the kind of *power* a group has to offset whatever polarization tendencies it might have. First—and importantly—the question of what a group can *do* not to polarize in an epistemically inappropriate way is constrained ex ante by what Lackey

(2014), along with List and Pettit (2011), call the *group/member action principle*.

> **Group/Member Action Principle (GMAP):** for every group, G and act, A, G performs A only if at least one member of G performs some act or other that causally contributes to A.

GMAP simply makes explicit that anything a group might do to overcome epistemically inappropriate polarization must itself emerge from some action or actions taken by individual members of the group (or at least some individual member of the group). But, of course, the satisfaction of this necessary condition on group action captured by GMAP is not sufficient for group action, and this is because a group acts *only if* (as per the Gilbert/Fricker model) suitable joint commitments to action are in place. What these observations imply is that what a group can do to mitigate tendencies to epistemically bad polarization is to make certain kinds of *joint commitments*, commitments individuals make as a group, and so the crucial issue we want to explore from this point forward is: which joint commitments will most effectively offset the epistemic pitfalls of group polarization?[1] What shape will such commitments take? How might they be implemented?

One approach to answering these questions is to take into account factors that empirical research singles out as contributing to group depolarization (see Chapter 2). Accordingly, one way to devise the joint commitments that could effectively offset the epistemic pitfalls of group polarization consists in inferring them, albeit indirectly, from the main theories of group polarization in the psychological literature. In particular, this empirically based approach to joint commitments can be summarized as follows:

> **JC:** if empirical theory T says that factor F leads or contributes to group polarization, the joint commitment that group members should adopt can be plausibly conceived as a commitment to suppress or avoid F.

Albeit empirically based, JC is a normative proposal, in that it suggests what members of a group *should* do in order for the group to depolarize (or not polarize). It is nonetheless a proposal with empirical reach, insofar as the relevant joint commitments can be subject to empirical testing and subsequent revision.

However, there is a problem with JC. As argued before, the idea is not that groups should never polarize (or that should always depolarize if they have polarized) but rather that they should not polarize *in an epistemically bad way*. Thus, while one virtue of JC is that it is in line with empirical theories of group polarization and depolarization, the downside is that it is unable to discriminate factors that lead or contribute to epistemically inappropriate polarization from those that do not. Accordingly, a more nuanced proposal would be this:

> **JC***: if empirical theory *T* says that factor *F* leads or contributes to group polarization and *F* is such that it leads or contributes to epistemically inappropriate group polarization, the joint commitment that group members should adopt can be then plausibly construed as a commitment to suppress or avoid *F* on the proviso that such a commitment promotes—or at least does not subvert—the reliable achievement of (one or more of) the goals that are constitutive of virtuous group polarization—namely: the evidential filtering, the evidential assessment, the non-epistemic influences filtering, and the evidential scrutiny goals.

The idea, in a nutshell, is this: whatever causes group polarization, if one such cause runs counter any of the goals that are constitutive of epistemically virtuous group polarization, group members should jointly commit to suppressing or avoiding such a factor but only if by doing so they do not bring further epistemic disvalue to the group (e.g., subverting the reliable achievement of any of the other epistemic goals).

We will illustrate how JC* can be put to work in the next sections. For the moment, though, recall the central tenets of the three main psychological theories of the mechanisms driving group polarization. According to *persuasive arguments theory*, group polarization is caused by the impact of informational exchanges on group members during collective deliberation and, in particular, by the fact that, during group discussion, they are exposed to new information in the direction of their own positions, which are thus reinforced. For *social comparison theory*, group polarization occurs when group members re-adjust their individual beliefs to a more extreme collective view due to social comparison mechanisms meant to avoid social censure or to obtain social approval. Finally, *self-categorization theory* holds that a process of self-categorization among group members produces group polarization; in particular, group members conform to a more extreme collective view trying to preserve their distinctiveness from other groups.

We can already anticipate the following point concerning the joint commitments that, we think, group members should adopt to avoid the epistemic pitfalls of group polarization. According to social comparison and self-categorization theory, the kinds of factors that cause group polarization are *non-epistemic*. As such, group members should jointly commit to suppressing or avoiding them altogether; the reason, as we saw in Chapter 3, is that it suffices that such non-epistemic factors are in place to render the way a group polarizes epistemically inadequate. By contrast, the kinds of factors that persuasive arguments theory posits as causes of group polarization are *epistemic* (namely, informational or evidential). Accordingly, group members should jointly commit to suppressing or avoiding them *only if* they are bad epistemic factors, i.e., factors that contribute to epistemically improper group polarization.

9.2 An Anti-deliberation Commitment?

Before proposing relevant joint commitments groups can adopt to avoid polarizing in an epistemically vicious way, let's consider a provocative proposal that has recently appeared in the philosophical literature first. In a recent paper by Brian Hedden (2017), one very strong such commitment is canvassed and defended in the special case of juries: a commitment to *non-deliberation*. In particular, Hedden argues that the various deleterious effects of jury deliberation jointly justify a mandatory *non-deliberation policy* for jurors that limits the information available to jurors and constrains their decision-making powers, with the aim of increasing accuracy.

We remain skeptical that, even if a non-deliberation policy, framed more generally (i.e., not exclusively in the case of juries), was effective at mitigating epistemically deleterious effects of group polarization, groups *should*, from an epistemic point of view, jointly commit to such a non-deliberation policy.

One reason is that deliberation typically generates various kinds of clear epistemic benefits—e.g., pooling of evidence (Hong & Page 2012); positive effects on juror memory (Vollrath et al. 1989; cf., Pritchard & Keenan 2002)—and this is the case even though, when a group polarizes, such benefits are characteristically defeated (i.e., by being overridden by documented epistemically disvaluable consequences of the polarizing effect).

Another reason, related to the previous, is this. If deliberation is suppressed, groups do not polarize (or only slightly polarize).[2] While group polarization can be epistemically appropriate or inappropriate (see Chapter 3), the latter occurs more often, but the former occurs in the very best epistemic circles, such as science, academic research, or expertise more generally. Moreover, in such circles, epistemically appropriate group polarization is epistemically *valuable* in that it makes the groups involved come closer to the truth in their inquiries. Therefore, suppressing deliberation, by preventing epistemically appropriate group polarization, also prevents epistemically valuable inquiry in the best epistemic circles.

This does not imply that Hedden is not right in thinking that a non-deliberation policy should be the norm in the case of juries specifically. Our claim is that a non-deliberation policy should not generalize to all contexts where group deliberation can be beneficial—especially to those in which the groups involved have the highest epistemic credentials (experts)—on pain of incurring epistemic losses, including missed opportunities of epistemic improvement. Therefore, ceteris paribus, a group with a shared goal of mitigating epistemically inappropriate group polarization will be better off than a non-deliberative group by jointly committing to policies that achieve this goal without also foregoing the epistemic benefits made possible by deliberation, to the extent that such a strategy is feasible.

We think there is cause to be optimistic here. In what follows, we want to outline four key kinds of joint-commitments that can together serve—and without simply excising deliberation simpliciter—to fruitfully minimize epistemically bad polarization effects: these are (i) *group structural commitments*; (ii) *evidential commitments*; (iii) *anti-social comparison commitments*; and (iv) *anti-self-categorization commitments*.

9.3 Group Structural Commitments

If a necessary condition for group polarization is that individual members are like-minded, one plausible way to depolarize a group is by *increasing its diversity*, especially during deliberation. Groups that are jointly committed to being diverse enough in their membership and inclusive in internal deliberation impose on their members certain practical and epistemic obligations (see, e.g., Gilbert 2006: 147) that, when collectively realized, can undermine enabling conditions for lack of inclusiveness during deliberation. Practically, groups jointly committed to diversity will be committed to exercising both "forward-looking" and "backward-looking" controls on group structure. For example, in the former case, the group's joint commitment requires checks on any additional members to be added to the group, so as to guarantee or at least contribute to group diversity. Crucially, the effectiveness of these forward-looking joint commitments will depend on what is understood by diversity.

Diversity can be understood in (at least) two ways: (i) difference in opinion and (ii) difference in competence or ability.[3] Now, while adopting a joint commitment to diversity, understood as per (i), can plausibly depolarize a group—since groups whose members disagree polarize less—it is unclear that the group will be thereby in a better epistemic position. In particular, increasing diversity in opinion before deliberation can, in some cases, lead to mistaken collective views following deliberation, i.e., views that would have been correct otherwise. For example, consider a group of scientists who individually believe, competently, drawing on the best scientific evidence, that Earth is not flat but an oblate spheroid. If, before group discussion, half of the scientists are replaced with scientifically untrained flat-Earthers, the group, as a result, might not polarize after group discussion—it would become starkly divided instead—but this does not obviously translate into an epistemic improvement. The revamped group is simply not epistemically better off than when only the scientists competently polarize toward believing what is true: that Earth is not flat.

A different kind of forward-looking joint commitment to diversity that groups might do well to adopt is a commitment to include members with diverse abilities in the deliberative process before it takes place. Arguments for more inclusive deliberation, understood as per (ii), are often given by advocates of deliberative democracy (e.g., Landemore 2012), drawing on several formal results such as the "Diversity Trumps Ability Theorem", which informally says that, given certain conditions, "a randomly selected collection of problem solvers outperforms a collection of the best individual problem solvers" (Page 2007: 162);[4] the Diversity Prediction Theorem, i.e., the idea that a "crowd's collective accuracy equals the average individual accuracy minus their collective predictive diversity" (Page 2007: 197), viz., the idea that ability matters as much as diversity in predictive tasks; or different jury theorems, such as the Condorcet Jury Theorem, which states that given two possible options concerning a given topic (e.g., a verdict, a diagnosis, a factual issue), where only one of the options is correct (viz., true), the probability that a majority votes for the correct option increases and converges to one as the size of the group grows.[5]

Although these and related theorems definitely bolster the idea that more inclusive deliberation is desirable from an epistemic point of view, they do not apply to all kinds of groups,[6] and to the extent that this is the case, different groups might be epistemically better off (vis-à-vis preventing or mitigating epistemically vicious group polarization) by making different kinds of forward-looking group structural commitments, e.g., to:

- Increasing the group's diversity (in Page's sense).
- Increasing the group's size (as per Condorcet reasons).
- Increasing the group's number of experts.
- Decreasing the group's number of incompetent members.

In sum, steering clear of epistemically vicious group polarization might require different kinds of *forward-looking controls* and corresponding group structural commitments depending on factors such as the size of the group or the degree of individual ability of its members—such commitments are not necessarily incompatible. In general, the question of what groups should do—vis-à-vis group structure—in order to achieve epistemically optimal results in general (i.e., not just to prevent epistemically vicious group polarization) is, to a large extent, an open question in several areas of philosophy as well as in different empirical and formal disciplines, with two general opposing lines of thought: those who think that better epistemic results are achieved by (i) larger groups of *diverse* problem-solvers, voters, etc. and those who think that (ii) smaller groups of *experts* perform epistemically better.[7] We do not intend to adjudicate between these two general tenets: the collective virtue/vice model, predicated on the idea of joint commitment (to greater diversity or expertise) is compatible with both (in the case of group polarization) as well as with implementing the specific proposals that advocates of each have offered.

In the case of *backward-looking controls*, the relevant joint commitments are retrodictive in that they will involve changes to the group structure already in place in light of facts about current demographics. Realizing such a joint commitment will involve *reshaping* the current group structure whenever certain relevant demographics are overrepresented. In the simplest kind of case of reshaping, where the independent aim of satisfying a minimum capacity on group membership is not threatened by the realization of a joint commitment to diversity or expertise, this will involve a commitment to requiring that certain members exit the group—a commitment to be clear that those individuals whose group membership is ultimately revoked will have *themselves* agreed to previously by jointly committing to fostering ingroup diversity or expertise.

Where the loss of group members undermines a minimum capacity commitment, this will involve a commitment to *replacing* extant individual members with new members either randomly or arbitrarily following epistemic criteria (e.g., replacing someone without expertise on pandemics with someone holding a PhD in epidemiology; someone who has not taken [or has failed] the Bar exam with a practicing lawyer; individuals without proven experience in an area of inquiry with individuals with a solid track-record; etc.) or else in accordance with non-epistemic criteria (e.g., replacing a conservative with a liberal [or vice versa]; a man with a woman [or vice versa]; an individual making over $100,000 a year with someone making less than $100,000 per year [or vice versa], etc.).

In addition, reshaping may not only be a matter of replacement but also take the form of *adding* new members randomly or arbitrarily following epistemic or non-epistemic criteria. When this is done in large numbers (e.g., as it happens in online communities), the groups in question can potentially obtain better epistemic results (such as avoidance of epistemically vicious group polarization) if Condorcet-style theorems apply. But, of course, large groups (e.g., online communities, voters) can still polarize in epistemically bad ways. Whether this happens or not is, to a large extent, an empirical question.

Finally, whereas the practical obligations associated with both forward-looking and backward-looking group structural joint commitments are reorganizational, these will naturally be complemented by epistemic obligations to forward-looking and backward-looking *epistemic vigilance*, namely a commitment to monitoring (and if required, updating) current group membership demographics relevant to the practical obligations vis-à-vis new membership and reshaping.

The foregoing kinds of joint commitments with respect to group structure can do additional "anti-polarizing" work. In particular, because polarization entrepreneurs and otherwise dogmatic individuals have (as we have previously noted) the effect of facilitating epistemically vicious polarization, group structural commitments can include commitments that limit or exclude such individuals. At this point, a natural question is whether group structural commitments, broadly construed as commitments to regulating group membership, might *suffice* to undermine (or at least significantly mitigate) epistemically vicious group polarization. Evidence-based reasons suggest a negative answer.

To bring this point into sharp relief, consider the concrete example of jury selection in the case of criminal law, where prevailing norms include the provision of attorney challenges—viz., opportunities for attorneys on both sides to disqualify an individual from the jury on the grounds that the individual is unable or unlikely to be suitably impartial in her evaluation of the evidence. Assume, ex hypothesi, that typical controls for such impartiality have been exercised through the normal attorney challenge procedure and, even further, that potential jurors and attorneys agree to more extreme measures tailored to controlling for ingroup homogeneity—viz., that what is committed to is the legitimacy of attorney challenges not *merely* in usual cases of perceived partiality as recognized in criminal law (e.g., as typical reasons for dismissing jurors) but also in cases where admitting otherwise impartial potential jurors would lead to the exceeding of demographics thresholds not directly related to partiality as such.

Now consider that even in such a hypothesized case where group structure is controlled for in a more or less ideal way, evidence cited by proponents of persuasive arguments theory suggests that factors responsible for group polarization might nonetheless remain, and this is because the kind of *informational influences* that persuasive arguments theory highlights as a cause of group polarization will not necessarily be eliminated simply in virtue of controlling just for the kinds of individuals represented within the group. To the extent that such informational influences might involve, e.g., bad evidence being distributed within the group, which is a factor that, as we have seen, contributes to epistemically vicious polarization, mere group structural commitments will not suffice for preventing it. Evidence distribution is, after all, a factor that is independent of diversity of membership. Moreover, even granting membership only to experts will not suffice to ward off the kind of informational influences that trigger epistemically vicious group polarization. For example, if misleading evidence is not properly filtered out of group discussion—or if the experts in question, albeit competent at seeing the confirmational import of the evidence, are not particularly reliable at seeking for possible good counterevidence against the group's dominant view—epistemically bad polarization ensues. Accordingly, while joint commitments to controlling for group structure with an eye to diversity or expertise can control for some factors typically responsible for epistemically inadequate group polarization, further kinds of joint commitments are needed.

9.4 Evidential Commitments

Recall that, according to persuasive arguments theory, the main cause of group polarization is the informational exchanges that take place during group discussion and, in particular, that individuals are often disproportionately exposed to and attend to evidence that favors the position to which they were antecedently leaning. This, we've argued, is not necessarily epistemically bad. Only good evidence can be discussed by competent members, who, as a result of such informational influences, virtuously polarize. And as we've also seen, there are three central *evidential* factors that can contribute to making polarization epistemically vicious: not achieving reliably the (i) evidential filtering, (ii) the evidential assessment, and (iii) the evidential scrutiny goals; that is, when groups are unreliable at (i) filtering out bad evidence of group discussion; (ii) correctly assessing the confirmational import of the group's private and shared evidence; or (iii) searching, discussing, and correctly assessing good counterevidence against the beliefs of individual members (when there is an epistemic obligation to do it), as well as examining the most plausible ways to potentially disprove such beliefs. We submit that an antidote to this residual problem would be to adopt joint commitments to evidential policies aimed at meeting—or at least facilitating the achievement of—such goals. In what follows, we will survey a range of such joint commitments that we take to be promising.

First, though, note that, according to the collective (viz., non-reductionist) virtue/vice model, group members do not need to be individually competent at meeting these evidential goals for group polarization to be epistemically virtuous—as the group itself can be competent due to the use of collective methods—but being individually competent can be sufficient for virtuous polarization provided that the group is also competent at meeting the non-epistemic influences filtering goal (see §8.2.4 for some examples). This has the following implication: the evidential policies group members can jointly commit to so as to overcome—or at least mitigate—epistemically vicious group polarization are of two kinds: (i) *individually oriented* and (ii) *group-oriented*. These are not incompatible policies, and, in some cases, groups might commit to evidential policies that involve individual and collective measures.

Consider, for instance, the evidential filtering goal. One individually oriented joint commitment members of a deliberative group can adopt is to ensure that all members participating in group discussion achieve a minimum degree of competence at filtering the bad evidence, i.e., at ruling out as "bad" evidence coming from unreliable methods and untrustworthy sources. This joint commitment can be put into practice in several ways. For example, group members can commit to receiving proper training, such as training on how to distinguish trustworthy sources from untrustworthy ones (e.g., peer-reviewed journals from obscure or predatory publishers) or reliable from unreliable methods (e.g., meta-analyses, randomized clinical trials, cohort studies, etc. from patient observations, homeopathic methods, etc.) or more technical training on, e.g., experimental design, to be able to tell, competently, whether experimental results are valid and reliable.[8] If this is not possible, members incompetent at filtering out bad evidence can still jointly commit to deferring to the group's experts, and such expert members can correspondingly commit to taking up this task. Where none of this is possible (but also complementarily), group members can adopt group-oriented joint commitments, such as the commitment to use software that distinguishes the good from the bad evidence by identifying trustworthy sources and reliable methods or the commitment to rely on external expert reports.

The same kinds of considerations and joint commitments apply to the evidential assessment and evidential scrutiny goals. By adopting such kinds of individually and group-oriented commitments (viz., individual training, deference to the group's experts, dedicated software, external expert reports) groups can thereby be in a better epistemic position to correctly assess the confirmational import of the group's private and shared evidence (*evidential assessment goal*) as well as to search, discuss, and correctly assess good counterevidence against the beliefs of individual members (when there is an epistemic obligation to do it) and to examine the most plausible ways to prove such beliefs wrong (*evidential scrutiny goal*). It is by adopting these kinds of joint commitments that groups can be competent at meeting the three relevant evidential goals and thus be in a position to avoid epistemically vicious group polarization.

In addition, one final kind of evidential joint commitment related to the *dynamics* of group deliberation might be still needed, which is to make sure that arguments and evidence (for multiple positions) are not only distributed equally and thus not asymmetrically throughout the group prior to reaching consensus or a group's view but also that individuals engage with arguments and evidence relatively equally. Against the background of our preferred version of the Gilbert/Fricker framework articulated in Chapter 8, this latter "equality of engagement" commitment will involve of individuals that each of them give consideration to (perhaps by spending an equal amount of time and effort analyzing) arguments for and against one's previously held position *provided others are willing to do the same*. Such a joint commitment, undertaken by the group as a body, might plausibly go further than merely structural commitments in controlling for the key problem highlighted by persuasive argument theory—which is that individuals are exposed to more arguments favoring their own position—and attend primarily to these.

9.5 Anti-social Comparison Commitments

In previous sections, we've proposed ways in which a group can collectively act to avoid polarizing in an epistemically bad way—either by depolarizing in the right epistemic way or by ensuring that the group becomes competent at securing the goals that are apposite to epistemically virtuous group polarization—specifically via joint commitments that explicitly control for the kind of empirically established causes of group polarization which, we think, have negative epistemic status. Group structural commitments and evidential commitments of the sort sketched go a long way toward this goal. However, it will be valuable, vis-à-vis the aim of avoiding epistemically vicious group polarization, for individuals to jointly commit to courses of action that can control for causes of polarization associated with social comparison theory, the crucial claim of which is that (in cases of polarization) individuals evaluate their own opinions and abilities by comparison with others' opinions and abilities—perceiving and presenting themselves in ways that are socially desirable to others—to the point that they are inclined to adopt more extreme views during group discussion to avoid social censure or obtain social approval.

Note that such tendencies can persist independently of either (i) group structural controls (as per §9.3); or (ii) controls on evidential filtering, assessment, scrutiny, or on distribution of and engagement with arguments and evidence (as per §9.4). As we saw in Chapter 2, psychological studies on depolarizing mechanisms indicate that, as we would expect, eliminating opportunity conditions for such social comparison has a depolarizing effect. Recall, for example, Abrams and colleagues' studies (1990), which show that providing conditions for *private* responses by group members decreases ingroup influence, and that, when categorical differences between subgroups within a discussion group are made salient, convergence of opinion between the subgroups is inhibited (Abrams 1990: 113–114).

Naturally, joint commitments aimed at facilitating (i) privacy contexts and (ii) a lack of salience (e.g., blindness or anonymity) of categorical differences between members will accordingly be instrumental toward a group's more general aim of preventing non-epistemic factors from influencing group deliberation (i.e., toward the *non-epistemic influences filtering goal* epistemically virtuous groups are competent at). But what concrete shape should such commitments take? Here the most promising proposal we believe will incorporate elements of John Rawls' (1971) well-known "veil of ignorance" thought experiment. Note that *even if* facts about categorical differences between individual subgroups are not actually made explicitly salient, a residual problem is that various individual biases (e.g., prestige bias, stereotyping, etc.) might nonetheless contribute to making such categorical differences *implicitly salient*, at least in circumstances where individuals have access to some identifying information about other group members. Even with such collateral information, individuals can jointly commit to acting as members of the group under a "veil of ignorance" in the following way: by operating (e.g., deliberating) as group members *as if* (and provided others operate/deliberate as if) which viewpoints are socially approved within the group is unknown. Or, alternatively, that *whether* the viewpoint that any given individual leans toward will be socially accepted is a matter that is established randomly. The joint commitment of individual group members to such a useful fiction would have the consequence of undermining some of the enabling conditions that, with reference to social comparison theory, give rise to epistemically vicious group polarization.

However, there is perhaps a setback. While (as per Gilbert) joint commitments are defined as *conditional commitments* (i.e., commitments individuals have insofar as other group members fulfill their commitments), the fulfillment conditions of typical commitments are *publicly verifiable* in ways that the previously suggested Rawlsian joint commitment would not be. As a consequence, the possibility of mitigating epistemically vicious group polarization through the vehicle of this kind of commitment will likely be realized only in certain kinds of communities of trust (e.g., Alfano 2016)—viz., communities that have antecedently satisfied certain epistemic conditions on social cohesion (e.g., Dunbar 1993, 2005).

9.6 Anti-self-categorization Commitments

Even if individuals are jointly committed to controlling for social comparison via the kinds of mechanisms suggested in §9.5, individuals might nonetheless be influenced by pressures to forge a *social identity* in virtue of their participation in the deliberating group and in such a way that typically involves minimizing intragroup differences and maximizing intergroup differences (Turner 1982; Turner et al. 1989). Plausibly, any joint commitment to undercut conditions for social identity formation will have to be a joint commitment to both pre-deliberation and post-deliberation intra- and inter-group anonymity. While a joint commitment to such anonymity might seem impractical or practically impossible without jettisoning deliberation entirely (as per Hedden's suggestion), current technologies have removed what would have previously been obvious barriers to the realization of such commitments.

In particular, the MeetingSift collaborative software platform, for example, allows meeting participants to exchange ideas (e.g., to deliberate) entirely anonymously. The New York State Society of Certified Public Accounts, having used this software in group decision making, attests that it makes possible group deliberation in conditions "without the fear of rejection, to achieve consensus that is free from political influence". Likewise, The Association for Women in Science (AWIS) has also praised anonymous voting conditions as ones that encourage "individual members to express their true preference rather than voting with the group, as influenced by political or social dynamics".[9] Joint commitments to deliberating under such conditions would have obvious anti-epistemically vicious-polarization import insofar as realizing such a commitment will imply that the salient enabling conditions for social identity fostering (e.g., recognition of inter- and intra-group differences) will have been effectively eliminated—or at least substantially minimized. Furthermore, unlike the kind of Rawlsian proposal sketched in §9.5, a commitment to deliberating under conditions of anonymity is a commitment the satisfaction conditions for which are publicly verifiable, in part due to technologies like MeetingSift. Accordingly, a joint commitment to deliberative anonymity could be realized not exclusively in communities of trust but also in populations exhibiting generalized mistrust and lack of social cohesion.

Notes

1. Of course, it is always possible that for any given joint commitment to *A*, the group, in fact, does not *A* successfully despite jointly committing to *A*. Granting this is compatible with appreciating that such joint commitments may be the best policy for limiting or mitigating epistemically inadequate group polarization, even if not *immunizing* the group from its possibility.
2. Cf. Teger and Pruitt (1967) for a study on polarization effects after exposing group members to other members' views absent group discussion.
3. The latter interpretation is in line with Scott E. Page's understanding of diversity (Page 2007) as cognitive (not personality) differences. Page specifies this broad understanding of the notion of diversity with four further distinctions: cognitive differences as (i) different ways of representing situations and problems, i.e., of seeing or envisioning the set of possible solutions to a problem differently (*diverse perspectives*); (ii) different ways of categorizing or partitioning perspectives, i.e., the different categories people use to classify events, outcomes, and situations (*diverse interpretations*); (iii) different ways of generating solutions to problems, from simple rules of thumb to sophisticated analytic techniques (*diverse heuristics*); and (iv) different ways of inferring cause and effect, of describing causal relationships between objects or events (*diverse predictive models*). See Page (2007: 7–9) for examples of (i)–(iv).
4. Page helpfully explains the rationale behind the Diversity Trumps Ability Theorem as follows:

    The best problem solvers tend to be similar; therefore, a collection of the best problem solvers performs little better than any one of them individually. A collection of random, but intelligent, problem solvers tends to be diverse. This diversity allows them to be collectively better. Or to put it more provocatively: *diversity trumps ability*.

    (Page 2007: 137)

5. See Dietrich and Spiekermann's (2020) for a useful epistemology-oriented overview of jury theorems.
6. For example, here is Page contrasting the Diversity Trumps Ability Theorem with the "Diversity Prediction Theorem":

    In making a prediction, a group of randomly selected predictors might or might not predict more accurately than a group of the best predictors. Randomly selected predictors will be more diverse, to be sure, but they will also be less accurate. The two effects work in opposite directions. So, we cannot expect that a random intelligent group will predict more accurately than the group of the best.

(Page 2007: 208–209)

Or consider the Condorcet Jury Theorem, which is premised upon two demanding conditions: that the probability (viz., reliability) that each group member identifies the correct position is higher than 0.5 and the same for all voters (voter competence condition) and that all correct votes are mutually independent conditional on the truth.

7. For example, the tension between these two options is evidenced in the disagreement held between advocates of the epistemic turn in deliberative democracy (cf., Landemore 2017), i.e., the idea that there are correct answers in politics (cf., Estlund 2003) and that large deliberative majorities are able to track them—and advocates of epistocracy (e.g., Brennan 2016), the idea that only people with sufficient political knowledge or competence ought to be the bearers of political power.

8. For a recent overview of some of these kinds of training strategies, see, e.g., Sharma et al. (2019).

9. See http://meetingsift.com/anonymity-success-factor-for-group-decision-making/.

Conclusion
Future Directions

So where have we gotten to? In one sense, we've hopefully come a long way. Over the course of this book, we've defended clear answers to the guiding questions about the metaphysics and epistemology of group polarization with which we started out.

On the metaphysics side, we've argued that group polarization— understood as a phenomenon that affects the epistemic lives of groups— *cannot* be reduced to epistemic features of their individual members. If our argument succeeds, then this tells us something new about the nature of group polarization, which takes us beyond any of the purely descriptive characterizations of group polarization that have been reached so far in empirical social psychology.

On the epistemology side, we've argued that group polarization is best understood in terms of an epistemic virtue/vice model as opposed to a cognitive heuristics/bias model. Putting these two conclusions together, we get the combined result that group polarization is best understood as a feature that, when instantiated by a group, is irreducibly instantiated and that that feature that the group irreducibly instantiates is neither a (group-level) heuristic nor a (group-level) bias but, rather, a (group-level) epistemic virtue or vice.

So, which is it then? Is group polarization a collective epistemic virtue or a collective epistemic vice? The point of Chapter 3 was to clarify why it is that a question like this (though prima facie reasonable) is wrongheaded, in that it rests on the mistaken idea that group polarization is epistemically good or bad, per se. We've shown, contrary to this idea, that (and in short) it is the epistemic status of the factors that make groups polarize that turns group polarization into an epistemically good or bad phenomenon, and these factors can differ significantly across polarization contexts. Accordingly, the view defended can preserve that pretheoretically plausible idea that while it might not be epistemically vicious for ideal Bayesian agents to polarize, it can *and often times is* epistemically vicious when, in more common cases, our social media debates lead us to become more entrenched than previously. Our reasons for treating the former case as epistemically virtuous polarization and the latter as epistemically vicious polarization are principled and grounded in a detailed examination of the ways that groups can—from an epistemic point of view—do better or worse when attempting to reach a conclusion.

The overarching view advanced, we've shown, achieves all of the best aspects of other potential combinations of construing the metaphysics and epistemology of group polarization while, at the same time, avoiding the costs that plague all the other salient alternative views. Establishing this comparative cost/benefit result has been a "slow-burning plot" (see the Scoreboard at the end of Chapter 8 for a summary). That said, we think that presenting this kind of "cross-combination" comparison in a systematic and organized way is really the only good way to see not only that (as we've argued) our proposed model of the metaphysics and epistemology of group polarization gets all the goods it does—but also without incurring the various sorts of baggage that other philosophical views group polarization take on. Finally, we've demonstrated—and this was the result of Chapter 9—how gaining for the first time a foothold on the metaphysics and epistemology of group polarization offers us a new vantage point when it comes to understanding how to mitigate the epistemic pitfalls of group polarization, appreciated for what it is and for why it's epistemically problematic (when it is).

Despite the headway made, we regard our own view more as an entry point than a bookend to the philosophy of group polarization. We've focused here on metaphysical and epistemological issues. These are not exhaustive. And so, by way of conclusion, we want to register three areas of research related to group polarization that have not been covered in any detail in this book but that nonetheless constitute what we think are promising lines for future *philosophical* research.

(i) *Group Polarization and Group Blame*

An important question in collective epistemology—and more generally, in the philosophy of groups—concerns group blame. In particular, when a group is collectively responsible for some problematic outcome, who should be held to account for it?[1]

A mostly uncontentious starting point is to say that some or all of the individuals of the group are to blame. But reductionist and non-reductionist approaches to group properties are committed to very different ways of making sense of this idea. A reductionist account on this score is simple: when a group polarizes in an epistemically problematic way, we blame the individual bad actors but not those group members whose individual behavior did not contribute to the epistemically problematic polarization. However, on the kind of non-reductive approach we favor, the situation is more complicated. After all, on our non-reductive view it looks as though blame for epistemically problematic polarization, a property of the group as a whole, will apply if at all to the group as a whole.

However—and here is a place where more work needs to be done. Consider an analogy with individual cognitive behavior. Not all problematic individual cognitive behavior is blameworthy behavior, even when things go wrong. Sometimes individuals have an *excuse*. When they do, they are not to be blamed.[2]

An important task for future research will, accordingly, be to theorize in a principled way about the conditions under which a group is blameworthy—or collectively excused—for polarizing in epistemically problematic way when it does. No such account presently exists.

(ii) *Political Ramifications*

Another topic in the philosophy of group polarization that merits more attention falls within the remit of political philosophy. It is a hallmark of liberal democracies that groups elect political leaders, that criminals accused of serious crimes are judged by groups, and that nearly all important policy decisions are subject to group vote. All of these group decisions, from jury verdicts, to senates and parliaments votes, to the electorate at large, are such that deliberation plays an important role in the process.

Is this for the best? Only very recently has this question been considered seriously in the negative, in the case of juries.[3] But the issue applies more widely. For those political philosophers who want to say "yes" to deliberation at all levels of group decision making, the very fact of group polarization forces important questions about responsible risk management. An interesting and mostly unexplored question concerns to what extent libertarian paternalist policies (e.g., Thaler & Sunstein 2008) such as nudging via choice architecture[4] might be reasonably implemented in response to epistemically problematic forms of group polarization without compromising values such as liberty and autonomy.

(iii) *Group Polarization and Collective Enhancement*

At the individual level, the latest technology and medicine offers new ways to improve our cognitive and intellectual capacities.[5] Traditionally, cognitive improvements have been undertaken *therapeutically*, viz., with the aim of correcting a defect or pathology so as to restore one to normal healthy levels of functioning. However, increasingly, medicine and technology—ranging from smart drugs, intelligence augmentation, and brain-computer interfaces—are used for purposes of cognitive *enhancement*, viz., to take individuals beyond healthy levels of functioning in order to gain various kinds of advantages.

Without exception, discussions of cognitive enhancement have taken place at the individual level, where the relevant issue is the improvement of individual cognitive functioning.[6]

But the identification of group polarization as an irreducibly collective phenomenon challenges this picture, particularly in those cases where polarization is epistemically vicious. Such cases invite a radical question: do the reasons we have for enhancing individual cognizers extend to group-level cognizers (including groups disposed to polarize in epistemically problematic ways), and if so, under what conditions? Moreover, how might the use of the latest technology and medicine to enhance (irreducibly) collective cognition differ from strategies that would be employed to enhance a group simply by improving the individual-level cognition of all or most of its members?

These questions—as well as the others just raised—challenge us to push the philosophy of group polarization in entirely new directions, with the hope of making headway beyond the progress we've managed here.

Notes

1. For several accounts of collective obligation and collective responsibility, see Isaacs (2011), Lawford-Smith (2012), and Collins (2013).
2. For an influential recent discussion of individual-level excuses, see Williamson (2016).
3. See, e.g., Hedden (2017).
4. For a recent discussion of nudging via choice architecture on the Internet, see Alfano et al. (2018).
5. For a review of these technologies, see Bostrom and Sandberg (2009).
6. See, for example, Savulescu and Bostrom (2009) and Carter and Pritchard (2019).

References

Abramowitz, A.I. and Saunders, K.L. 1998. Ideological Realignment in the U.S. Electorate. *The Journal of Politics* 60 (3): 634–652.

Abrams, D., Wetherell, M., Cochrane, S., Hogg, M.A., and Turner, J.C. 1990. Knowing What to Think by Knowing Who You Are: Self-Categorization and the Nature of Norm Formation, Conformity and Group Polarization. *British Journal of Social Psychology* 29: 97–119.

Alfano, M. 2012. Expanding the Situationist Challenge to Responsibilist Virtue Epistemology. *The Philosophical Quarterly* 62 (247): 223–249.

———. 2013. *Character as Moral Fiction*. Cambridge: Cambridge University Press.

———. 2014. Expanding the Situationist Challenge to Reliabilism about Inference. In A. Fairweather (ed.), *Virtue Epistemology Naturalized*. Dordrecht, NL: Springer: 103–22.

———. 2016. The Topology of Communities of Trust. *Russian Sociological Review* 15 (4): 30–56.

———. Forthcoming. Epistemic Situationism: An Extended Prolepsis. In M. Alfano and A. Fairweather (eds.), *Epistemic Situationism*. Oxford: Oxford University Press.

Alfano, M., Carter, J.A., and Cheong, M. 2018. Technological Seduction and Self-Radicalization. *Journal of the American Philosophical Association* 4 (3): 298–322.

Alfano, M. and Loeb, D. 2014. Experimental Moral Philosophy. In E.N. Zalta (ed.), *The Stanford Encyclopedia of Philosophy*. Summer.

Alston, W.P. 1995. How to Think about Reliability. *Philosophical Topics* 23 (1): 1–29.

Anscombe, G.E.M. 1957, June. XIV—Intention. In *Proceedings of the Aristotelian Society*, Vol. 57, No. 1. Oxford, UK: Oxford University Press: 321–332.

Argote, L., Seabright, M.A., and Dyer, L. 1986. Individual versus Group Use of Base-Rate and Individuating Information. *Organizational Behavior and Human Decision Processes* 38: 65–75.

Arvan, M. 2019. The Dark Side of Morality: Group Polarization and Moral Epistemology. *Philosophical Forum* 50: 87–115.

Baehr, J. 2009. Evidentialism, Vice, and Virtue. *Philosophy and Phenomenological Research* 78 (3): 545–567.

———. 2011. *The Inquiring Mind*. Oxford: Oxford University Press.

Bail, C.A., Argyle, L.P., Brown, T.W., Bumpus, J.P., Chen, H., Hunzaker, M.F., . . . and Volfovsky, A. 2018. Exposure to Opposing Views on Social Media Can Increase Political Polarization. *Proceedings of the National Academy of Sciences* 115 (37): 9216–9221.

Balcetis, E. and Dunning, D. 2006. See What You Want to See: Motivational Influences on Visual Perception. *Journal of Personality and Social Psychology* 91: 612–625.

Barba, M. and Broncano-Berrocal, F. *Manuscript*. Collective Epistemic Luck.

Barber, M. and McCarty, N. 2015. Causes and Consequences of Polarization. In N. Persily (ed.), *Solutions to Political Polarization in America*. Cambridge: Cambridge University Press: 15–58.

Battaly, H. 2014. Varieties of Epistemic Vice. In J. Matheson and R. Vitz (eds.), *The Ethics of Belief*. Oxford: Oxford University Press: 51–76.

———. 2015. *Virtue*. Cambridge, UK: John Wiley & Sons.

———. 2018. Closed-Mindedness and Dogmatism. *Episteme* 15 (3): 261–282.

Beebe, J.R. 2004. The Generality Problem, Statistical Relevance and the Tri-Level Hypothesis. *Noûs* 38 (1): 177–195.

Bird, A. 2010. Social Knowing: The Social Sense of "Scientific Knowledge." *Philosophical Perspectives* 24: 23–56.

———. 2014. When Is There a Group That Knows? In J. Lackey (ed.), *Essays in Collective Epistemology*. Oxford: Oxford University Press: 42–63.

———. 2019. Group Belief. In M. Fricker, P.J. Graham, D. Henderson, and N. Pedersen (eds.), The *Routledge Handbook of Social Epistemology*. Abingdon, UK: Routledge.

Bordley, R.F. 1983. A Bayesian Model of Group Polarization. *Organizational Behavior and Human Performance* 32 (2): 262–274.

Bostrom, N. and Sandberg, A. 2009. Cognitive Enhancement: Methods, Ethics, Regulatory Challenges. *Science and Engineering Ethics* 15 (3): 311–341.

Brady, M.S. and Fricker, M. (eds.). 2016. *The Epistemic Life of Groups: Essays in the Epistemology of Collectives*. Oxford: Oxford University Press.

Bramson, A., Grim, P., Singer, D.J., Berger, W.J., Sack, G., Fisher, S., Flocken, C., and Holman, B. 2017. Understanding Polarization: Meanings, Measures, and Model Evaluation. *Philosophy of Science* 84: 115–159.

Bray, R.M. and Noble, A.M. 1978. Authoritarianism and Decisions of Mock Juries: Evidence of Jury Bias and Group Polarization. *Journal of Personality & Social Psychology* 36 (12): 1424–1430.

Brennan, J. 2016. *Against Democracy*. Princeton: Princeton University Press.

Broncano-Berrocal, F. 2017. A Robust Enough Virtue Epistemology. *Synthese* 194: 2147–2174.

———. 2018. Purifying Impure Virtue Epistemology. *Philosophical Studies* 175: 385–410.

Broncano-Berrocal, F. and Carter, J.A. 2017. Epistemic Luck. In *Routledge Encyclopedia of Philosophy Online*. Abingdon, UK: Routledge.

———. Forthcoming. Deliberation and Group Disagreement. In F. Broncano-Berrocal and J.A. Carter (eds.), *The Epistemology of Group Disagreement*. Abingdon, UK: Routledge.

Brown, R. 1986. *Social Psychology: The Second Edition*. New York: The Free Press.

Brownstein, M. and Saul, J. (ed.). 2016. *Implicit Bias and Philosophy*, Vol. 1 and 2. Oxford: Oxford University Press.

Bruder, M., Haffke, P., Neave, N., Nouripanah, N., and Imhoff, R. 2013. Measuring Individual Differences in Generic Beliefs in Conspiracy Theories across Cultures: Conspiracy Mentality Questionnaire. *Frontiers in Psychology* 4: 225.

Burnstein, E. and Vinokur, A. 1977. Persuasive Argumentation and Social Comparison as Determinants of Attitude Polarization. *Journal of Experimental Social Psychology* 13 (4): 315–332.

Carter, J. Adam; Gordon, Emma C. & Jarvis, Benjamin (eds.) (2017). Knowledge First: Approaches in Epistemology and Mind. Oxford: Oxford University Press.

Carter, J., and McKenna, R. (2020). Skepticism Motivated: On the Skeptical Import of Motivated Reasoning. *Canadian Journal of Philosophy* 50 (6): 702–718. doi: 10.1017/can.2020.16

Carter, J.A., Jarvis, B.W., and Rubin, K. 2016. Belief Without Credence. *Synthese* 193 (8): 2323–2351.

Carter, J.A. and Pritchard, D.H. 2019. The Epistemology of Cognitive Enhancement. *The Journal of Medicine and Philosophy* 44 (2): 220–242.

Cassam, Q. 2015. Bad Thinkers. *Aeon.* https://aeon.co/essays/the-intellectual-character-of-conspiracy-theorists.

———. 2016. Vice Epistemology. *The Monist* 99 (2): 159–180.

———. 2018. Epistemic Insouciance. *Journal of Philosophical Research* 43: 1–20.

———. 2019. *Vices of the Mind.* Oxford: Oxford University Press.

Chemero, A. 2009. *Radical Embodied Cognitive Science.* Cambridge, MA: MIT Press.

Clark, A. and Chalmers, D.J. 1998. The Extended Mind. *Analysis* 58 (1): 7–19.

Coady, D. (ed.). 2006. *Conspiracy Theories: The Philosophical Debate.* Farnham, UK: Ashgate Publishing, Ltd.

Cohen, G.L. 2003. Party over Policy: The Dominating Impact of Group Influence on Political Beliefs. *Journal of Personality and Social Psychology* 85: 808–822.

Collins, S. 2013. Collectives' Duties and Collectivisation Duties. *Australasian Journal of Philosophy* 91: 231–248.

Conee, E. and Feldman, R. 1998. The Generality Problem for Reliabilism. *Philosophical Studies* 89 (1): 1–29.

Crawford, J.T. 2012. The Ideologically Objectionable Premise Model: Predicting Biased Political Judgments on the Left and Right. *Journal of Experimental Social Psychology* 48: 138–151.

Crerar, C.B. 2017. Motivational Approaches to Intellectual Vice. *Australasian Journal of Philosophy.* ISSN 0004-8402

Del Vicario, M., Scala, A., Caldarelli, G. et al. 2017. Modeling Confirmation Bias and Polarization. *Scientific Reports* 7: 40391. https://doi.org/10.1038/srep40391.

Del Vicario, M., Vivaldo, G., Bessi, A. et al. 2016. Echo Chambers: Emotional Contagion and Group Polarization on Facebook. *Scientific Reports* 6: 37825. https://doi.org/10.1038/srep.

Dietrich, F. and Spiekermann, K. 2020. Jury Theorems. In M. Fricker (ed.), *The Routledge Handbook of Social Epistemology.* New York and Abingdon, UK: Routledge.

Ditto, P.H., Pizarro, D.A., and Tannenbaum, D. 2009. Motivated Moral Reasoning. In D.M. Bartels, C.W. Bauman, J.L. Skitka, and D.L. Medin (eds.), *The Psychology of Learning and Motivation*, Vol. 50. Cambridge, MA: Academic Press: 307–338.

Doris, J.M. 1998. Persons, Situations, and Virtue Ethics. *Noûs* 32 (4): 504–530.

———. 2002. *Lack of Character: Personality and Moral Behavior.* Cambridge: Cambridge University Press.

Dunbar, R.I. 1993. Coevolution of Neocortical Size, Group Size and Language in Humans. *Behavioral and Brain Sciences* 16 (4): 681–694.

———. 2005. Gossip in Evolutionary Perspective. *Review of General Psychology* 8 (2): 100–110.

Egan, A. 2008. Seeing and Believing: Perception, Belief Formation and the Divided Mind. *Philosophical Studies* 140 (1): 47–63.

Estlund, D. 2003. Why Not Epistocracy? In N. Reshotko (ed.), *Desire, Identity and Existence: Essays in Honor of T. M. Penner*. Canada: Academic Printing and Publishing: 53–69.

Evans, J.St.B.T. 2003. In Two Minds: Dual-Process Accounts of Reasoning. *Trends in Cognitive Sciences* 7: 454–459.

Felton, D. 1973. The Dangers of Charisma: Mel Lyman and Fort Hill. In *Communes: Creating and Managing the Collective Life*. New York: Harper and Row.

Festinger, L. 1954. A Theory of Social Comparison Processes. *Human Relations* 7: 117–140.

Fiorina, M.P. and Abrams, S.J. 2008. Political Polarization in the American Public. *Annual Review of Political Science* 11: 563–588.

Fraser, C., Gouge, C., and Billig, M. 1971. Risky Shifts, Cautious Shifts, and Group Polarization. *European Journal of Social Psychology* 1: 7–30.

Fricker, M. 2010. Can There Be Institutional Virtues? *Oxford Studies in Epistemology* 3: 223–235.

Froese, T., Gershenson, C., and Rosenblueth, D.A. 2013. *The Dynamically Extended Mind*. http://arxiv.org/abs/1305.1958.

Frost, K. 2014. On the Very Idea of Direction of Fit. *Philosophical Review* 123 (4): 429–484.

Gigerenzer, G. and Goldstein, D.G. 1996. Reasoning the Fast and Frugal Way: Models of Bounded Rationality. *Psychological Review* 103 (4): 650.

Gigerenzer, G., Todd, P.M., and the ABC Research Group. 1999. *Simple Heuristics that Make Us Smart*. New York: Oxford University Press.

Gilbert, M. 1987. Modelling Collective Belief. *Synthese* 73 (1): 185–204.

———. 1989. Rationality and Salience. *Philosophical Studies* 57 (1): 61–77.

———. 2000. *Sociality and Responsibility: New Essays in Plural Subject Theory*. London: Rowman and Littlefield.

———. 2006. *A Theory of Political Obligation: Membership, Commitment, and the Bonds of Society*. Oxford: Oxford University Press on Demand.

———. 2013. *Joint Commitment: How We Make the Social World*. New York: Oxford University Press.

———. 2017. Joint Commitment. In *The Routledge Handbook of Collective Intentionality*. Abingdon, UK: Routledge: 130–139.

Goethals, G.R. and Zanna, M.P. 1979. The Role of Social Comparison in Choice Shifts. *Journal of Personality and Social Psychology* 37: 1469–1476.

Goldberg, S.C. 2016. On the Epistemic Significance of Evidence You Should Have Had. *Episteme* 13 (4): 449–470.

———. 2017. Should Have Known. *Synthese* 194 (8): 2863–2894.

Goldman, A. 1988. Strong and Weak Justification. *Philosophical Perspectives* 2: 51–69.

———. 1999. *Knowledge in a Social World*. Oxford: Oxford University Press.

———. 2014. Social Process Reliabilism: Solving Justification Problems in Collective Epistemology. In J. Lackey (ed.), *Essays in Collective Epistemology*. Oxford: Oxford University Press: 11–41.

Goldstein, D.G. 2009. Heuristics. In P. Hedström and P. Bearman (eds.), *The Oxford Handbook of Analytical Sociology*. New York: Oxford University Press: 140–164.

Goldstein, D.G. and Gigerenzer, G. 2002. Models of Ecological Rationality: The Recognition Heuristic. *Psychological Review* 109: 75–90.

Greco, J. 1999. Agent Reliabilism. *Philosophical Perspectives* 13: 273–296.

———. 2003. Knowledge as Credit for True Belief. In M. DePaul and L. Zagzebski (eds.), *Intellectual Virtue: Perspectives from Ethics and Epistemology.* Oxford: Oxford University Press: 111–134.

———. 2010. *Achieving Knowledge.* Cambridge: Cambridge University Press.

———. Forthcoming. The Transmission of Knowledge and Garbage. *Synthese.*

Hacking, I. 1982. Language, Truth and Reason. In M. Hollis and S. Lukes (eds.), *Rationality and Relativism.* Cambridge, MA: MIT Press: 48–66.

Harman, G. 1999. Moral Philosophy Meets Social Psychology: Virtue Ethics and the Fundamental Attribution Error. *Proceedings of the Aristotelian Society* 99: 315–331.

———. 2000. The Nonexistence of Character Traits. *Proceedings of the Aristotelian Society* 100: 223–226. Wiley Online Library.

Haidt, J. 2001. The Emotional Dog and Its Rational Tail: A Social Intuitionist Approach to Moral Judgment. *Psychological Review* 108: 814–834.

Haidt, J., Rosenberg, E., and Hom, H. 2003. Differentiating Diversities: Moral Diversity Is Not Like Other Kinds. *Journal of Applied Social Psychology* 33: 1–36.

Hallsson, B.G. Forthcoming. The Epistemic Significance of Political Disagreement. *Philosophical Studies.*

Hedden, B.R. 2017. Should Juries Deliberate? *Social Epistemology* 2017: 1–19. doi: 10.1080/02691728.2016.1270364.

Hetherington, M.J. 2009. Review Article: Putting Polarization in Perspective. *British Journal of Political Science* 39 (2): 413–448.

Hibbing, J.R., Smith, K.B., and Alford, J.R. 2014. Differences in Negativity Bias Underlie Variations in Political Ideology. *Behavioral and Brain Sciences* 37: 297–307.

Hinsz, V.B., Tindale, R.S., and Nagao, D.H. 2008. Accentuation of Information Processes and Biases in Group Judgments Integrating Base-Rate and Case-Specific Information. *Journal of Experimental Social Psychology* 44 (1): 116–126.

Hollingshead, A.B. 1998a. Retrieval Processes in Transactive Memory Systems. *Journal of Personality and Social Psychology* 74 (3): 659.

———. 1998b. Communication, Learning, and Retrieval in Transactive Memory Systems. *Journal of Experimental Social Psychology* 34 (5): 423–442.

Hollingshead, A.B. and Brandon, D.P. 2003. Potential Benefits of Communication in Transactive Memory Systems. *Human Communication Research* 29 (4): 607–615.

Hong, L. and Page, S. 2012. Some Microfoundations for Collective Wisdom. In H. Landemore and J. Elster (eds.), *Collective Wisdom: Principles and Mechanisms.* Cambridge: Cambridge University Press.

Hourihan, K.L. and Benjamin, A.S. 2010. Smaller Is Better (When Sampling from the Crowd within: Low Memory-Span Individuals Benefit More from Multiple Opportunities for Estimation. *Journal of Experimental Psychology: Learning, Memory, and Cognition* 36 (4): 1068–1074.

Humberstone, I.L. 1992. Direction of Fit. *Mind* 101 (401): 59–83.

Hutchins, E. 1995. *Cognition in the Wild.* Cambridge, MA: MIT press.

Isaacs, T. 2011. *Moral Responsibility in Collective Contexts.* Oxford: Oxford University Press.

Isenberg, D.J. 1986. Group Polarization: A Critical Review and Meta-Analysis. *Journal of Personality and Social Psychology* 50 (6): 1141–1151.

Iyengar, S. and Westwood, S.J. 2015. Fear and Loathing across Party Lines: New Evidence on Group Polarization. *American Journal of Political Science* 59: 690–707.

Jellison, J.M. and Riskind, J. 1970. A Social Comparison of Abilities Interpretation of Risk Taking Behavior. *Journal of Personality and Social Psychology* 15 (4): 375–390.

Kahan, D.M. 2013. Ideology, Motivated Reasoning, and Cognitive Reflection. *Judgment and Decision Making* 8: 407–424.

Kahan, D.M., Hoffman, D.A., Braman, D., Evans, D., and Rachlinski, J.J. 2012. They Saw a Protest: Cognitive Illiberalism and the Speech-Conduct Distinction. *Stanford Law Review* 64: 851–906.

Kahan, D.M., Jenkins-Smith, H., and Braman, D. 2011. Cultural Cognition of Scientific Consensus. *Journal of Risk Research* 14: 147–174.

Kahan, D.M., Peters, E., Dawson, E.C., and Slovic, P. 2017. Motivated Numeracy and Enlightened Self-Government. *Behavioural Public Policy* 1: 54–86.

Kahneman, D. 2003. Maps of Bounded Rationality: Psychology for Behavioral Economics. *American Economic Review* 93: 1449–1475.

———. 2011. *Thinking, Fast and Slow*. London: Penguin UK.

Kallestrup, J. 2016. Group Virtue Epistemology. *Synthese*: 1–19. doi: 10.1007/s11229-016-1225-7.

Keeley, B.L. 1999. Of Conspiracy Theories. *The Journal of Philosophy* 96 (3): 9–126.

Kelly, J.R., McCarty, M.K., and Iannone, N.E. 2013. Interaction in Small Groups. In J. DeLamater and A. Ward (eds.), *Handbook of Social Psychology*, 2nd ed. Dordrecht, NL: Springer.

Kelly, T. 2008. Disagreement, Dogmatism, and Belief Polarization. *Journal of Philosophy* 105 (10): 611–633.

Kelp, C. 2014. Two for the Knowledge Goal of Inquiry. *American Philosophical Quarterly* 51 (3): 227–232.

Kentridge, R.W. 2011. Attention without Awareness. In C. Mole, D. Smithies, and W. Wu (eds.), *Attention: Philosophical and Psychological Essays*. Oxford: Oxford University Press.

Klayman, J. 1995. Varieties of Confirmation Bias. *Psychology of Learning and Motivation* 32: 385–418.

Krizan, Z. and Baron, R.S. 2007. Group Polarization and Choice-Dilemmas: How Important Is Self-Categorization? *European Journal of Social Psychology* 37: 191–201.

Kruglanski, A.W. 2004. *The Psychology of Closed Mindedness*. London: Psychology Press.

Kunda, Z. 1990. The Case for Motivated Reasoning. *Psychological Bulletin* 108: 480–498.

Lackey, J. 2014. Socially Extended Knowledge. *Philosophical Issues* 24 (1): 282–298.

Lahroodi, R. 2007. Collective Epistemic Virtues. *Social Epistemology* 21 (3): 281–297.

Lamm, H. and Myers, D.G. 1978. Group-Induced Polarization of Attitudes and Behavior. In L. Berkowitz (ed.), *Advances in Experimental Social Psychology*, Vol. 2. New York: Academic Press: 147–195.

Landemore, H. 2012. *Democratic Reason: Politics, Collective Intelligence, and the Rule of the Many*. Princeton: Princeton University Press.

———. 2017. Beyond the Fact of Disagreement? The Epistemic Turn in Deliberative Democracy. *Social Epistemology* 31 (3): 277–295.

Lane, T. and Liang, C. 2011. Self-Consciousness and Immunity. *Journal of Philosophy* 108: 78–99.

Lawford-Smith, H. 2012. The Feasibility of Collectives' Action. *Australasian Journal of Philosophy* 90: 453–467.

Layman, G.C., Carsey, T.M., and Horowitz, J.M. 2006. Party Polarization in American Politics: Characteristics, Causes, and Consequences. *Annual Review of Political Science* 9: 83–110.

Leiserowitz, A.A. 2005. American Risk Perceptions: Is Climate Change Dangerous? *Risk Analysis* 25: 1433–1442.

Lelkes, Y. 2016. Mass Polarization: Manifestations and Measurements. *Public Opinion Quarterly* 80 (1): 392–410.

Levendusky, M.S. 2013. *How Partisan Media Polarize America*. Chicago: University of Chicago Press.

Levinger, G. and Schneider, D.J. 1969. Test of the "Risk Is a Value" Hypothesis. *Journal of Personality and Social Psychology* 11 (2): 165–169.

Levy, N. 2005. The Good, the Bad, and the Blameworthy. *Journal of Ethics and Social Philosophy* 1 (2): 1–16.

———. Forthcoming. Virtue Signalling Is Virtuous. *Synthese*: 1–18.

Libet, B., Gleason, C.A., Wright, E.W., and Pearl, D.K. 1983. Time of Conscious Intention to Act in Relation to Onset of Cerebral Activity (Readiness-Potential): The Unconscious Initiation of a Freely Voluntary Act. *Brain* 106: 623–642.

List, C. and Pettit, P. 2006. Group Agency and Supervenience. *Southern Journal of Philosophy* 44: 85–105.

———. 2011. *Group Agency: The Possibility, Design, and Status of Corporate Agents*. Oxford: Oxford University Press.

Liu, B.S. and Ditto, P.H. 2013. What Dilemma? Moral Evaluation Shapes Factual Belief. *Social Psychological and Personality Science* 4: 316–323.

Lord, Charles, G., Ross, L., and Lepper, M. 1979. Biased Assimilation and Attitude Polarization: The Effects of Prior Theories on Subsequently Considered Evidence. *Journal of Personality and Social Psychology* 37 (11): 2098–2109.

Lyons, J. Forthcoming. Algorithm and Parameters: Solving the Generality Problem for Reliabilism. *Philosophical Review*.

Main, E.C. and Walker, T.G. 1973. Choice Shifts and Extreme Behavior: Judicial Review in the Federal Courts. *Journal of Social Psychology* 91: 215–221.

Mandelbaum, E. 2016. Attitude, Inference, Association: On the Propositional Structure of Implicit Bias. *Noûs* 50 (3): 629–658.

Marx, S.M., Weber, E.U., Orlove, B.S., Leiserowitz, A., Krantz, D.H., Roncoli, C., and Phillips, J. 2007. Communication and Mental Processes: Experiential and Analytic Processing of Uncertain Climate Information. *Global Environmental Change-Human and Policy Dimensions* 17: 47–58.

McCauley, C., Stitt, C.L., Woods, K., and Lipton, D. 1973. Group Shift to Caution at the Race Track. *Journal of Experimental Social Psychology* 9 (1): 80–86.

McHoskey, J.W. 1995. Case Closed? On the John F. Kennedy Assassination: Biases Assimilation of Evidence and Attitude Polarization. *Basic and Applied Social Psychology* 17: 395–409.

Medina, J. 2013. *The Epistemology of Resistance: Gender and Racial Oppression, Epistemic Injustice, and the Social Imagination.* New York: Oxford University Press.

Mercier, H. 2011. When Experts Argue: Explaining the Best and the Worst of Reasoning. *Argumentation* 25 (3): 313–327.

Mercier, H. and Sperber, D. 2017. *The Enigma of Reason.* Cambridge, MA: Harvard University Press.

Miller, A.G., McHoskey, J.W., Bane, C.M., and Dowd, T.G. 1993. The Attitude Polarization Phenomenon: Role of Response Measure, Attitude Extremity, and Behavioral Consequences of Reported Attitude Change. *Journal of Personality and Social Psychology* 64 (4): 561–574.

Montmarquet, J.A. 1993. *Epistemic Virtue and Doxastic Responsibility.* London: Rowman and Littlefield.

Moscovici, S. and Zavalloni, M. 1969. The Group as a Polarizer of Attitudes. *Journal of Personality & Social Psychology* 12 (2): 125–135.

Mullen, E. and Nadler, J. 2008. Moral Spillovers: The Effect of Moral Violations on Deviant Behavior. *Journal of Experimental Social Psychology* 44: 1239–1245.

Munro, G.D. and Ditto, P.H. 1997. Biased Assimilation, Attitude Polarization, and Affect in Reactions to Stereotyped-Relevant Scientific Information. *Personality and Social Psychology Bulletin* 23: 636–653.

Murray, I., Plagnol, A., and Corr, P. 2017, September 24. *When Things Go Wrong and People Are Afraid: An Evaluation of Group Polarisation in the UK Post Brexit.* https://ssrn.com/abstract=3041846 or http://dx.doi.org/10.2139/ssrn.3041846.

Myers, D.G. 1975. Discussion-Induced Attitude Polarization. *Human Relations* 28 (8): 707–711.

———. 2010. Group Polarization. In J.M. Levine and M.A. Hogg (eds.), *Encyclopedia of Group Processes and Intergroup Relations.* Thousand Oaks, CA: Sage Publications.

Myers, D.G. and Bishop, G.D. 1970. Discussion Effects on Racial Attitudes. *Science* 169 (3947): 778–779.

Myers, D.G. and Kaplan, M.F. 1976. Group-Induced Polarization in Simulated Juries. *Personality and Social Psychology Bulletin* 2 (1): 63–66.

Myers, D.G. and Lamm, H. 1975. The Polarizing Effect of Group Discussion. *American Scientist* 63: 297–303.

———. 1976. The Group Polarization Phenomenon. *Psychological Bulletin* 83: 602–607.

Nam, H.H., Jost, J.T., and Bavel, J.J.V. 2013. "Not for All the Tea in China!" Political Ideology and the Avoidance of Dissonance. *PLoS One* 8: 8.

Nguyen, C.T. 2018. Echo Chambers and Epistemic Bubbles. *Episteme*: 1–21.

Nickerson, R.S. 1998. Confirmation Bias: A Ubiquitous Phenomenon in Many Guises. *Review of General Psychology* 2 (2): 175–220.

Nucci, L.P. 2001. *Education in the Moral Domain.* Cambridge: Cambridge University Press.

O'Connor, C. and Weatherall, J.O. 2017. Scientific Polarization. *European Journal for Philosophy of Science* 8: 855–875.

Olsson, E.J. 2013. A Bayesian Simulation Model of Group Deliberation and Polarization. In F. Zenker (ed.), *Bayesian Argumentation*, Synthese Library. Dordrecht, NL: Springer-Verlag.

————. Forthcoming. Why Bayesian Agents Polarize. In F. Broncano-Berrocal and J.A. Carter (eds.), *The Epistemology of Group Disagreement*. Abingdon, UK: Routledge.

Orejan, J. 2011. *Football/Soccer: History and Tactics*. Jefferson, NC: McFarland.

Page, S.E. 2007. *The Difference: How the Power of Diversity Creates Better Groups, Firms, Schools, and Societies*. Princeton: Princeton University Press.

Palermos, S.O. 2011. Belief-Forming Processes, Extended. *Review of Philosophy and Psychology* 2 (4): 741–765.

————. 2014. Loops, Constitution, and Cognitive Extension. *Cognitive Systems Research* 27: 25–41.

————. 2016. The Dynamics of Group Cognition. *Minds and Machines* 26 (4): 409–440.

————. 2017. Social Machines: A Philosophical Engineering. *Phenomenology and the Cognitive Sciences* 16 (5): 953–978.

Pallavicini, J., Hallsson, B., and Kappel, K. Forthcoming. Polarization in Groups of Bayesian Agents. *Synthese*.

Paulus, P.B. and Dzindolet, M.T. 1993. Social Influence Processes in Group Brainstorming. *Journal of Personality and Social Psychology* 64: 575–586.

Plantinga, A. 1993. *Warrant and Proper Function*. Oxford: Oxford University Press.

Pomerantz, E.M., Chaiken, S., and Tordesillas, R.S. 1995. Attitude Strength and Resistance Processes. *Journal of Personality and Social Psychology* 69: 408–419.

Prinz, J. 2011. Is Attention Necessary and Sufficient for Consciousness? In C. Mole, D. Smithies, and W. Wu (eds.), *Attention: Philosophical and Psychological Essays*. Oxford: Oxford University Press.

Pritchard, D. 2005. *Epistemic Luck*. Oxford: Oxford University Press.

————. 2010. Cognitive Ability and the Extended Cognition Thesis. *Synthese* 175 (1): 133–151.

————. 2014. Re-Evaluating the Situationist Challenge to Virtue Epistemology. In A.

Pritchard, M.E. and Keenan, J.M. 2002. Does Jury Deliberation Really Improve Jurors' Memories? *Applied Cognitive Psychology: The Official Journal of the Society for Applied Research in Memory and Cognition* 16 (5): 589–601.

Pruitt, D.G. 1971. Choice Shifts in Group Discussion: An Introductory Review. *Journal of Personality and Social Psychology* 20 (3): 339–360.

Rabbie, J.M. and Visser, L. 1972. Bargaining Strength and Group Polarization in Intergroup Negotiations. *European Journal of Social Psychology* 2: 401–416.

Rawls, J. 1971. *A Theory of Justice*. Cambridge, MA: Harvard University Press.

Reimer, T. and Hoffrage, U. 2006. The Ecological Rationality of Simple Group Heuristics: Effects of Group Member Strategies on Decision Accuracy. *Theory and Decision* 60: 403–438.

Reimer, T. and Katsikopoulos, K. 2004. The Use of Recognition in Group Decision-Making. *Cognitive Science* 28: 1009–1029.

Robson, J. 2014. A Social Epistemology of Aesthetics: Belief Polarization, Echo Chambers and Aesthetic Judgement. *Synthese* 191: 2513–2528.

Rydell, R. and McConnell, A. 2006. Understanding Implicit and Explicit Attitude Change: A Systems of Reasoning Analysis. *Journal of Personality and Social Psychology* 91 (6): 995–1008.

Sanders, G.S. and Baron, R.S. 1977. Is Social Comparison Irrelevant for Producing Choice Shifts? *Journal of Experimental Social Psychology* 13: 303–314.

Savulescu, J. and Bostrom, N. (eds.). 2009. *Human Enhancement*. Oxford: Oxford University Press on Demand.

Schkade, D., Sunstein, C.R., and Kahneman, D. 2000. Deliberating about Dollars: The Severity Shift. *Columbia Law Review* 100 (4): 1139–1175.

Schulz-Hardt, S., Frey, D., Lüthgens, C., and Moscovici, S. 2000. Biased Information Search in Group Decision Making. *Journal of Personality and Social Psychology* 78 (4): 655.

Sharma, K., Qian, F., Jiang, H., Ruchansky, N., Zhang, M., and Liu, Y. 2019. Combating Fake News: A Survey on Identification and Mitigation Techniques. *ACM Transactions on Intelligent Systems and Technology* (TIST) 10 (3): 1–42.

Sherman, D.K. and Cohen, G.L. 2006. The Psychology of Self-Defense: Self-Affirmation Theory. *Advances in Experimental Social Psychology* 38: 183–242.

Siegel, S. and Zajonc, R.B. 1967. Group Risk Taking in Professional Decisions. *Sociometry* 30: 339–349.

Simion, M., Kelp, C., and Ghijsen, H. 2016. Norms of Belief. *Philosophical Issues* 26 (1): 374–392.

Simon, H.A. 1982. *Models of Bounded Rationality*, 2 Vol. Cambridge, MA: MIT Press.

Singer, D.J., Bramson, A., Grim, P., Holman, B., Jung, J., Kovaka, K., Ranginani, A., and Berger, W.J. Forthcoming. Rational Social and Political Polarization. *Philosophical Studies*.

Skitka, L.J., Bauman, C.W., and Mullen, E. 2008. Morality and Justice: An Expanded Theoretical Perspective and Review. In K.A. Hedgvedt and J. Clay-Warner (eds.), *Advances in Group Processes*, Vol. 25. Bingley, UK: Emerald Group Publishing Limited: 1–27.

Skitka, L.J., Bauman, C.W., and Sargis, E.G. 2005. Moral Conviction: Another Contributor to Attitude Strength of Something More? *Journal of Personality and Social Psychology* 88: 895–917.

Smart, P.R. 2016. *Mandevillian Intelligence: From Individual Vice to Collective Virtue*. Socially-Extended Knowledge. Oxford, UK: Oxford University Press.

———. 2018. Mandevillian Intelligence. *Synthese* 195 (9): 4169–4200.

Smart, P.R., Huynh, T.D., Braines, D., and Shadbolt, N.R. 2010. Dynamic Networks and Distributed Problem-Solving. In *Knowledge Systems for Coalition Operations*. Vancouver, BC, Canada. https://eprints.soton.ac.uk/271508/1/Dynamic_Networksv3.pdf.

Sosa, E. 1991. *Knowledge in Perspective: Selected Essays in Epistemology*. Cambridge: Cambridge University Press.

———. 2009. *A Virtue Epistemology: Apt Belief and Reflective Knowledge*, Vol. 1. Oxford: Oxford University Press.

———. 2015. *Judgment and Agency*. Oxford: Oxford University Press.

Stahlberg, D., Eller, F., Maass, A., and Frey, D. 1995. We Knew It All Along: Hindsight Bias in Groups. *Organizational Behavior and Human Decision Processes* 63: 46–58.

Stanovich, K.E. and West, R.F. 2000. Individual Differences in Reasoning: Implications for the Rationality Debate? *Behavioral and Brain Sciences* 23: 645–665.

Stasser, G. and Titus, W. 1985. Pooling of Unshared Information in Group Decision Making: Biased Information Sampling during Discussion. *Journal of Personality and Social Psychology* 48: 1467–1478.

Stoner, J.A.F. 1961. *A Comparison of Individual and Group Decision Involving Risk*. Unpublished master's thesis, Massachusetts Institute of Technology.

Sunstein, C.R. 1999. The Law of Group Polarization. University of Chicago Law School, John M. Olin Law & Economics Working Paper (91).

———. 2000. Deliberative Trouble? Why Groups Go to Extremes. *The Yale Journal* 110 (1): 71.

———. 2002. The Law of Group Polarization. *Journal of Political Philosophy* 10: 175–195.

———. 2006a. Deliberating Groups vs. Prediction Markets (or Hayek's Challenge to Habermas). *Episteme* 3: 192–213.

———. 2006b. Misfearing: A Reply. *Harvard Law Review* 119: 1110–1125.

———. 2009. *Going to Extremes: How Like Minds Unite and Divide*. Oxford: Oxford University Press.

———. 2014. *Conspiracy Theories and Other Dangerous Ideas*. New York: Simon and Schuster.

———. 2016. *The Ethics of Influence: Government in the Age of Behavioral Science*. Cambridge: Cambridge University Press.

Sunstein, C.R. and Vermeule, A. 2009. Conspiracy Theories: Causes and Cures. *The Journal of Political Philosophy* 17 (2): 202–227.

Sutton, J., Harris, C.B., Keil, P.G., and Barnier, A.J. 2010. The Psychology of Memory, Extended Cognition, and Socially Distributed Remembering. *Phenomenology and the Cognitive Sciences* 9 (4): 521–560. doi: 10.1007/s11097-010-9182-y.

Tanesini, A. 2016. "Calm Down Dear": Intellectual Arrogance, Silencing and Ignorance. *Aristotelian Society: Supplementary Volume* 90 (1): 71–92.

———. 2018. Collective Amnesia and Epistemic Injustice. In J.A. Carter, A. Clark, J. Kallesrup, D. Pritchard, and S.O. Palermos (eds.), *Socially Extended Epistemology*. Oxford: Oxford University Press.

Teger, A.I. and Pruitt, D.G. 1967. Components of Group Risk Taking. *Journal of Experimental Social Psychology* 3: 189–205.

Tetlock, P.E., Kirstel, O.V., Elson, S.B., Green, M.C., and Lerner, J.S. 2000. The Psychology of the Unthinkable: Taboo Trade-Offs, Forbidden Base Rates, and Heretical Counterfactuals. *Journal of Personality and Social Psychology* 78: 853–870.

Thagard, P. 1993. Societies of Minds: Science as Distributed Computing. *Studies in History and Philosophy of Science* 24: 49–67.

Thaler, R.H. and Sunstein, C.R. 2008. *Nudge: Improving Decisions About Health, Wealth, and Happiness*. New Haven & London: Penguin.

Theiner, G. 2010. Making Sense of Group Cognition. In *ASCS09: Proceedings of the 9th conference of the Australasian Society for Cognitive Science*. Sydney, Australia: Macquarie Centre for Cognitive Science: 334–342.

Theiner, G. and O'Connor, T. 2010. The Emergence of Group Cognition. In A. Corradini and T. O'Connor (eds.), *Emergence in Science and Philosophy*. London: Routledge: 6–78.

Tollefsen, D. and Dale, R. 2011. Naturalizing Joint Action: A Process-Based Approach. *Philosophical Psychology* 25: 385–407.

Tollefsen, D.P. 2015. *Groups as Agents*. New York: John Wiley & Sons.

Tosi, J. and Warmke, B. 2016. Moral Grandstanding. *Philosophy and Public Affairs* 44: 197–217.

Tuomela, R. 1992. Group Beliefs. *Synthese* 91 (3): 285–318.

Turner, J.C. 1982. Towards a Cognitive Redefinition of the Social Group. In H. Tajfel (ed.), *Social Identity and Intergroup Relations*. Westport, CT: Praeger: 59–84.

Turner, J.C., Hogg, M.A., Oakes, P.J., Reicher, S.D., and Wetherell, M.S. 1987. *Rediscovering the Social Group: A Self-Categorization Theory*. London: Basil Blackwell.

Turner, J.C., Wetherell, M.S., and Hogg, M.A. 1989. A Referent Informational Influence Explanation of Group Polarization. *British Journal of Social Psychology* 28: 135–148.

———. Forthcoming. Knowledge as Achievement, More or Less. In M.A. Fernandez (ed.), *The Present and Future of Virtue Epistemology*. Oxford: Oxford University Press.

Tversky, A. and Kahneman, D. 1974. Judgment under Uncertainty: Heuristics and Biases. *Science*, New Series 185 (4157): 1124–1131.

Uhlmann, E., Pizarro, D.A., Tannenbaum, D., and Ditto, P.H. 2009. The Motivated Use of Moral Principles. *Judgment and Decision Making* 4: 476–491.

Vinokur, A. and Burnstein, E. 1978. Depolarization of Attitudes in Groups. *Journal of Personality and Social Psychology* 36 (8): 872–885.

Vollrath, D.A., Sheppard, B.H., Hinsz, V.B., and Davis, J.H. 1989. Memory Performance by Decision-Making in Groups and Individuals. *Organizational Behavior and Human Decision Processes* 43: 289–300.

Watson, G. 1996. Two Faces of Responsibility. *Philosophical Topics* 24 (2): 227–248.

Weber, E.U. and Stern, P.C. 2011. Public Understanding of Climate Change in the United States. *American Psychologist* 66: 315–328.

Wegner, D.M. 1986. Transactive Memory: A Contemporary Analysis of the Group Mind. In B. Mullen and G.R. Goethals (eds.), *Theories of Group Behavior*. New York: Springer-Verlag.

———. 1995. A Computer Network Model of Human Transactive Memory. *Social Cognition* 13 (3): 319–339.

———. 2002. *The Illusion of Conscious Will*. Cambridge, MA: MIT Press.

Wegner, D.M., Giuliano, T., and Hertel, P. 1985. Cognitive Interdependence in Close Relationships. In W.J. Ickes (ed.), *Compatible and Incompatible Relationships*. New York: Springer-Verlag: 253–276.

Weisberg, M. and Muldoon, R. 2009. Epistemic Landscapes and the Division of Cognitive Labor. *Philosophy of Science* 76 (2): 225–252.

———. 2007. *The Philosophy of Philosophy*. Oxford: Oxford University Press.

———. 2016. Justifications, Excuses, and Sceptical Scenarios. In F. Dorsch and J. Dutant (eds.), *The New Evil Demon*. Oxford: Oxford University Press.

———. 2019. *Doing Philosophy*. Oxford: Oxford University Press.

Wolf, S. 2019. Attributability and the Self. In *Oxford Studies in Agency and Responsibility Volume 5: Themes from the Philosophy of Gary Watson*, Vol. 5. Oxford: Oxford University Press: 38.

Woodside, A.G. 1972. Informal Group Influence on Risk Taking. *Journal of Marketing Research* 9: 223–225.

Wright, J.C., Cullum, J., and Schwab, N. 2008. The Cognitive and Affective Dimensions of Moral Conviction: Implications for Attitudinal and Behavioral Measures of Interpersonal Tolerance. *Personality and Social Psychology Bulletin* 34: 1461–1476.

Xu, B., Liu, R., and He, Z. 2016. Individual Irrationality, Network Structure, and Collective Intelligence: An Agent-Based Simulation Approach. *Complexity* 21 (S1): 44–54.

Yılmaz, O. and Saribay, A.S. 2016. An Attempt to Clarify the Link between Cognitive Style and Political Ideology: A Non-Western Replication and Extension. *Judgment and Decision Making* 11 (3): 287–300.

Zagzebski, L.T. 1996. *Virtues of the Mind: An Inquiry Into the Nature of Virtue and the Ethical Foundations of Knowledge*. Cambridge: Cambridge University Press.

Zollman, K.J. 2010. The Epistemic Benefit of Transient Diversity. *Erkenntnis* 72 (1): 17–35.

Zuckerman, E. 2019. QAnon and the Emergence of the Unreal. *Journal of Design and Science* (6): 1–15.

Index